Good Faith Politics

REDUCING TRIBALISM, STARTING FROM THE LEFT

Rasaan Hollis

Good Faith Politics is a work of nonfiction. Nevertheless, some names and personal characteristics of individuals have been changed in order to disguise identities. Any resulting resemblance to persons living or dead is coincidental and unintentional.

Copyright © 2024 by Rasaan Tito Lee Hollis

All rights reserved.

No portion of this book may be used or reproduced in any manner without written permission except in the case of brief quotations embodied in critical articles and reviews.

This publication is sold with the understanding that neither the author nor the publisher is engaged in rendering legal, investment, accounting, or other professional services.

The author and the publisher have taken care in the preparation of this book, but make no expressed or implied warranty of any kind and assume no responsibility for errors or omissions. No liability is assumed for incidental or consequential damages in connection with or arising out of the use of the information or programs contained herein.

Manufactured in the United States of America.

Identifiers:

LCCN 2024916877

ISBN 979-8-9901526-0-1 (paperback)
ISBN 979-8-9901526-1-8 (hardcover)
ISBN 979-8-9901526-2-5 (ebook)

Cover design: David Provolo

In honor of Aaron Stark's friend
I don't know your name, but I know your light

Contents

Preface vii

1. Tribalism, the Disease 1
    Creating Butterflies 4
    An Eye for Respect 7
    The Scientist's Spirituality 11

2. Bring the Light 17
    Good Afternoon 18
    I'm a Box 21
    We the People 25
    Divided We Fall 27

3. Check Your Bias 33
    Preaching to the Choir 35
    Intellectual Humility 38
    Mighty Convenience 40
    Don't Be a Bot 46
    Boiled Frog Problems 51

4. What Does Winning Look Like? 57
    Legislation over Feelings 61
    Put down the Sledgehammer 64
    The True Power of Science 70
    Reasonable People Can Disagree 76

5. Personal Contexts 85
    Social Contexts 89
    The Context Switching Superpower 91
    Negative Contexts 94

6. Societal Contexts 97
    Would You Have Owned Slaves? 98
    Multivariate Societal Contexts 102
    Empiricism and Rationalism 107
    What Can Normal Look Like? 113
    Religious Tolerance 122

7. **Being Wrong Has Consequences** 131
    From Fear to Hatred 133
    Generalizing the Individual .138
    Tryouts for the Math Team .140
    Not Wrong, Just Wrong. 148

8. **Inclusion 2.0** 157
    Don't Make Unnecessary Enemies. 158
    Don't Be a Zealot 166
    The Lesser of Two Evils 170
    Populists for the Wealthy 174

9. **Problems of Scale** 179
    Squatters 179
    Migrants 181
    Social Security. 186
    Common Interests 190

10. **Welcome to the Jungle**. 195
    Good Men 196
    Law, Biden, Citizen 202
    Superior Force. 206
    The Honorable Machiavellian 210
    State of the Jungle. 213

11. **Strength Before Weakness** 217
    Sticks and Stones 218
    The Fall of Men 220
    Compound Interest 225

12. **Finding Us**. 233
    The Ultimate Context. 235
    Holy Stardust 241

Index 251

Preface

The first novel I remember reading was *The Hostile Hospital* by Lemony Snicket. It was the eighth book in *A Series of Unfortunate Events*. Snicket was kind enough to caution us against reading the book. The first eight sentences all ended with the word STOP in capital letters like this—STOP. If you ignored all eight of them like I did, you deserved your fate. You had been warned. If you are considering your option to read *The Hostile Hospital*, STOP.

Fast-forward two and a half decades later, and I have *Good Faith Politics* in my hand. I can't in good faith recommend this book to you, to anyone, without a warning. Don't despair, it isn't as horrid as *The Hostile Hospital*; I wouldn't wish that nightmare upon my worst enemy. By the end of *Good Faith Politics*, your worst enemy may not be an enemy anymore. Perhaps he will be a friend. A scary thought indeed.

Tribalism is ripping apart the United States. It's happening in slow motion, and for years, I had just been watching it. Day after day, at each other's throats because we were at each other's throats yesterday. It's funny, but I'm crying laughing. As a citizen, I felt the need to do something about it.

So here I am. I'm not an author, but I'm an author. I'm not a politician; I'm too honest. I am a Democrat. This book is for Democrats. In this respect, I'll be preaching to the choir, though I doubt that they will like what I have to say. Tribalism doesn't require much brainpower to solve. It requires willpower. Sincerely attempting to understand people that we don't like, and are actively opposing.

Resisting tribalism is uncomfortable. As such, this book is uncomfortable. I'm holding the left responsible for this issue because I'm on the left. Besides, blaming the opposition is just more tribalism, isn't it? The following pages represent my attempt, in good faith, to bring the country together by improving the Democratic Party.

Conservatives and independents are more than welcome to read *Good Faith Politics*; just be aware that my writing assumes that the reader is a member of the left. If you don't want to engage in a series of unfortunate events that may end with you befriending your enemies, STOP.

1. Tribalism, the Disease

*"Science is not only compatible with spirituality;
it is a profound source of spirituality."*
– Dr. Carl Sagan

♫ *Soul to Squeeze* | Red Hot Chili Peppers

I didn't make it far into childhood before realizing that I needed to establish a kill policy. I define "killing" as ending another entity's life. By this definition, we're all killers. Use a disinfecting wipe, and you slaughter millions of bacteria. Spend an afternoon gardening, and you've likely killed a few handfuls of plants. Have a ham sandwich for lunch; a pig had to die for it.

Bacteria, plants, who cares? Pigs? It starts to get interesting. I used to light newspapers on fire with sunlight focused through a magnifying glass. A few ants fell victim as well. Before long, the fallen ants began to weigh on my conscience, so I stopped. I was fascinated by nature. I would catch a variety of insects, place them in spiderwebs, then watch and see if they could escape. Even that felt wrong, but I justified it internally by arguing that I was feeding the spiders.

One-off justification here, one-off justification there... I needed a kill policy. An objective framework I could consult to determine whether or not I'd be wrong for killing something. I didn't want to repeat the ant experience, where I killed a few, felt bad, then stopped. Going forward, I wanted to make the right decision in the first place.

Establishing a good kill policy is hard work. It was during this process that I came to understand how poor my instincts were. I figured I'd start with some easy examples. I knew that in my policy, killing people would be considered wrong. Why? My instinctive answer was, "Because we're human." Feels right, but if a pig were writing the kill policy, wouldn't she say it's wrong to kill pigs because she's a pig? Could I criticize her for it? Not without being a hypocrite.

I was uncertain whether or not it was wrong to kill pigs, but I was confident it would be wrong to kill cats and dogs. Again, why? Because we keep them as pets? Because puppies and kittens are cuter than piglets? The first reasons that came to mind, that felt intuitively right, weren't objective. They were biased.

Building my kill policy wasn't valuable because it helped me navigate the political issue of abortion. It was valuable because it taught me two things. That bias felt good, and that it was the default setting. If I hadn't taken the time to explicitly lay out a kill policy, my behavior would still be determined by my instincts. By my biases.

Tribalism can be thought of as an extension of bias. It's bias based on group identity. As a flavor of bias, it has the same fundamental characteristics. Tribalism is natural, it feels good, and it's the default setting for groups of people. If you don't explicitly think about it, you may not notice its influence. Being under the influence of tribalism lowers the quality of our thinking, and makes us less willing to change our minds. It's difficult for a mind to grow when it's not willing to change.

Politics often boils down to binary choices between two options. Should politicians vote for or against a given bill? Should we cast our ballot for the Democrat or for the Republican running for office? In binary choices, there are often pros and cons to each side, with long-term consequences that we can't predict. As such, I'm not here to prescribe the optimal policy position for every issue. I'm here to help people understand the dangers of tribalism, and provide a framework for resisting it.

Reducing tribalism is actually quite simple. Simple enough to be expressed in a single sentence.

Attempt to understand each other, in good faith.

By "good faith," I mean a state of sincere positivity. In life, knowing what to do is often the easy part. Want to lose weight? Eat healthier foods and exercise more. Want to do better in school? Spend more time studying. Want to advance your career? Work harder, grow your marketable skills, and network. Usually, the hard part isn't knowing what to do; it's mustering the will and discipline to do it. "Life hacks" are often a distraction from the fact that achieving your goals is going to require significant effort.

Reducing tribalism is my goal and, like Uncle Sam, I want you to help me. During my undergraduate studies, one of my theology professors taught a course that emphasized the distinction between orthodoxy and orthopraxis. Both share the common prefix *ortho*, which means "correct." The difference lies in the suffixes; *doxy* refers to beliefs, and *praxis* refers to practices or actions. His course was about prioritizing orthopraxis over orthodoxy. Correct actions over correct beliefs.

Likewise, the priority in *Good Faith Politics* is orthopraxis. If by the end of this book you walk away feeling more knowledgeable and scholarly, that's great. It doesn't mean much unless it's accompanied by the will to resist the tribal darkness that tempts us. We don't need experts in ivory towers to solve this problem. We need ordinary people to be stubbornly positive despite being surrounded by negativity.

Creating Butterflies

Why should we care enough to spend any of our limited energy trying to address tribalism? For two reasons. The first is that tribalism is more dangerous than it looks. The second is that we're more powerful than we think. Let's begin by exploring the dangerous part.

When we analyze deadly diseases, a metric we often look at is the fatality rate. This makes sense, but we often don't pay enough attention to the transmission rate. After all, for a disease to harm you, you have to catch it first. Sometimes having a high fatality rate is bad for transmission. The deceased don't tend to travel and infect others. The disease of tribalism isn't dangerous because of its fatality rate, but because of its transmission rate. It's not that tribalism eventually infects everyone; it eventually infects everything.

It's easy to make the mistake of thinking that the consequences of unchecked tribalism are largely physical. Mass shootings motivated by hate, political assassination attempts, a second civil war, and so on. These acts of violence are horrible, but this is only the "fatality rate" portion.

Tribalism is like a disease that targets the immune system. A weak immune system on its own isn't a fatal condition. It makes the common cold a fatal condition. Blundering foreign policy causes people to lose their lives. Blundering fiscal policy causes people to lose their livelihoods. Blundering tribalism causes people to lose their minds, and then they make decisions on foreign and fiscal policy.

What issue do you care about the most? Education? Immigration? Climate change? Whatever it is, adding tribalism to it will almost certainly make it worse. When problem *a* impacts problems *b–z*, you should probably address *a* first.

Even if we agree that tribalism is a high-priority problem to address, we won't take action unless we believe we can make a difference. Hesitance in this regard is understandable, but there is a silver lining. Tribalism, the disease, is contagious. We're powerful because the cure is contagious as well.

The *butterfly effect* is a concept describing the truth that a small change early in a series of events can lead to large changes later on. We're usually only aware of the first few consequences of our actions. However, the cause-and-effect chain of events doesn't end when we stop paying attention to it. The butterfly effect is powerful, extending infinitely into the future. Like most powerful things, it can be used in positive or negative ways.

To illustrate the magnitude of the butterfly effect, we'll explore the consequences of conversations between middle school students Ethan and Jesse. Ethan doesn't quite fit in with other students at his school. He's socially reserved, and his peers sometimes call him a "nerd." Jesse is a friendlier-than-average, otherwise normal kid. Though Jesse doesn't really relate to Ethan, she makes an effort to speak with him every now and then.

Jesse feels like she's doing something nice by occasionally chatting with Ethan, but she doesn't believe it's very significant. What she may not know is that without their talks, Ethan's life would have gone an entirely different direction.

Even with their conversations, Ethan had an unhappy childhood since he lacked respect from his peers. However, his small interactions with Jesse were enough to help him avoid a downward spiral into depression that would have severely damaged his self-esteem. Since Ethan was able to maintain his confidence with Jesse's help, he had the courage to ask his crush out on a date later in college. This would eventually lead to marriage and the creation of a happy family.

Neither of them is aware of how Ethan's life would have progressed without their talks. Jesse may have thought that she did x amount of good, brightening Ethan's day every now and then. That's what she could see. If she were fully aware of the consequences of her actions, she would know that she prevented a battle with depression, which allowed for the creation of an entire happy family. That's far greater than x. Such is the power of the butterfly effect.

In this hypothetical example, we assumed that Jesse's positive actions resulted in a net positive butterfly effect. In the real world, it doesn't always turn out that way. Sometimes doing positive things results in negative consequences. However, I believe this is the exception to the rule.

Tribalism is a contagious social problem with a contagious social solution. Ideally, we'll become part of the solution, amplifying our positivity with the power of the butterfly effect. The least we can do is try not to be part of the problem, creating negativity that spreads, scales, and impacts people we don't even know.

We're creating butterflies whether we like it or not. More than we'll ever be aware of. The question is, are they going to have a net positive or negative impact on society?

An Eye for Respect

Tribal behavior is part of human nature itself. My contemporaries who study tribalism from the perspectives of biology, sociology, and psychology arrive at the same conclusion, albeit from different scientific angles. What the majority of them promptly do next is some form of giving up. Either the answer is "we're doomed" or we're advised to accept tribalism and try to make it work on our behalf. The latter is just a more complicated way of saying "we're doomed" in the long run.

Yes, tribalism is part of the human condition. Yes, the consequences become more dangerous as we become more powerful. Yes, it's impossible to eradicate completely. Yes, tribalism has been and will yet be the cause of violence, wars, and the downfall of civilizations. No, these aren't enough reasons to give up hope.

Human nature is riddled with negative behaviors. Bullying, slavery, tyranny of the majority, greed, sexism, sex crimes, discrimination, corruption, etc. Tribalism is just another item on the list. Can we eradicate any of these issues completely? No, they're in our nature. Do we use that fact as an excuse to give up? No, and we shouldn't. Though we still have progress to make, we in the West have done a pretty good job on most of them, compared to the humans of history.

Why are most experts on tribalism so pessimistic? Because it's difficult to solve. The more difficult a problem is, the less likely people are to try to fix it. Challenge a man to do thirty push-ups, and he may give it a shot. Challenge him to do three thousand, and he probably won't do any at all. Addressing tribalism is hard, but is it that hard? To answer this question, we'll discuss a few different types of difficulty.

- **Cognitive difficulty:** These challenges test your ability to think logically, memorize large quantities of information, multitask, etc.
  - Examples: memorizing vocabulary in a foreign language, designing a new system, academic excellence

- **Competitive difficulty:** These challenges pit you in direct competition with others. Even if the activity is easy, only one person can be the best.
  - Examples: becoming the highest-rated chess player in your country, winning a race against your friends, becoming the valedictorian of your class

- **Will difficulty:** These challenges test your ability to do things that you don't want to do, or to get others to do things that they don't want to do.
  - Examples: sticking to a new diet, practicing to improve a skill, convincing your extended family to show up for a monthly dinner

Which type is the most difficult? There are arguments to be made for each one. For competitive difficulty, there are a limited number of winners, which seems challenging by definition. However, being the fastest in your household is much easier than being the fastest in the world, so the context matters. How you feel about cognitive difficulty largely depends on the characteristics of your unique mind. Many will think that competitive difficulty is more challenging than cognitive difficulty. This isn't the case if you hold yourself to a standard higher than your peers.

We don't often think about will difficulty, but it can be just as challenging as the other two. It's deceptive because at face value, it looks easy. Assume that you want a group of ten students to spend at least thirty minutes per night on their homework. You're not asking them to comprehend all of the material. You're not asking them to win any academic competitions. You're just asking them for thirty minutes of effort. Guess what, you're probably not going to get thirty minutes out of all ten of them. It seems easier than getting them to win an academic competition, but if you consistently fail at both, is it easier really?

Countless people make New Year's resolutions to work out x times per week for a year. If you crunch the numbers on how many of them stick to it for the entire year, maintaining the resolution could be less likely than becoming class valedictorian. Solving tribalism requires attempting to understand each other, in good faith. This isn't a mentally demanding, cognitive challenge. There isn't anything competitive about it. We can reduce tribalism if we can generate the will to do it.

What makes overcoming tribalism such a difficult test of will? To answer this question, I'd like to explore two aphorisms. They each bear truth on their own, but when examined together, they illuminate this unique challenge.

Aphorism 1: You have to give respect to get respect.
Aphorism 2: An eye for an eye makes the whole world blind.

If everyone waits for each other to give respect before giving it in return, there will be no respect. Someone has to create the first respect in order for the reciprocity to follow. This is difficult enough starting from a neutral position, creating respect from nothing. It's even harder to find the will to create respect from disrespect. To counter bad faith attacks with good faith open-mindedness. To resist tribalism, this is our task. The current political environment is anything but neutral. It's a highly charged storm of ad hominem insults, groupthink, and cynicism.

An eye for an eye feels right. It's the engine that perpetuates cycles of hatred. The most comfortable thing to do is practice an eye for an eye forever, plunging into the darkness like masochistic dance partners. An eye for respect, on the other hand, doesn't feel right at all. Not to most of us, anyway. The engine of hatred, formidable though it may be, only works when eyes are exchanged for eyes. When respect enters the engine, it begins to break down.

Instead of passing increasingly hostile disrespect back and forth until we come to blows or stop talking to each other, we should receive their disrespect, transform it, and then hand them respect back. They likely won't transform it again, and we'll be able to go back and forth amicably into the future. If you manage to pull this off, you've likely transformed a negative butterfly effect into a positive one.

Some people will be stuck on negativity and disrespect no matter what. That's OK. We don't have to reach everyone. We just have to start turning the tide. The left and the right shouldn't merely tolerate each other; we should talk to each other, in good faith. What happens when there is a series of respectful exchanges between people with different ideas but common interests? People on both sides learn that the other isn't as foolish or immoral as they thought. Some of them may even change their minds, which is a good thing. None of this requires good thinking. It requires goodwill.

Someone has to be the first to express goodwill. It would be convenient if our political adversaries were to do this work for us, but as history shows, we can't rely on that. There are statues depicting the Greek Titan Atlas bearing the weight of the world upon his shoulders. People want to help Atlas, but they can't help him if they don't see him. Acting in good faith is a sacrifice. In practice, it's difficult because it feels like a sacrifice for *them*. In reality, it's a sacrifice for *us*.

Acting with the courage of my convictions, I can't ask the right side of the aisle to bear this burden. We can't afford to wait for each other to show respect and good faith. This is why I'm asking my own political party to step up and make improvements.

I believe that we on the left can take the lead, making changes to turn down the temperature. We can be the party that takes the first step to solve the most consequential issue of our time. If this makes me appear to be a traitor to my own side, that's the cost of doing business. I'm happy to pay it, but I wouldn't mind splitting the bill.

The Scientist's Spirituality

Tribalism expresses itself in politics, but the problem is much deeper. It's a human phenomenon. Actually, it's even deeper than that; other animal species engage in tribal behavior as well. The better we understand ourselves, the better we'll understand tribalism. The better we understand tribalism, the better we're equipped to notice and resist it.

If tribalism is bias based on group identity, the tribe is the group that the bias is based on. In the political realm, Democrats and Republicans are tribes; so is the entire United States. In the religious realm, Baptists and Catholics are tribes; so is Christianity as a whole.

Tribalism is broader than politics, and exists at many levels of scale. Consequently, understanding it requires forays into political and nonpolitical disciplines. We'll seek wisdom from history, science, rhetoric, game theory, statistics, thought experiments, and parables. Wisdom will be our source of willpower for resisting tribalism.

During tests of will, pessimism is one of the most important barriers to overcome. In my experience, one's outlook on life is often a matter of juxtaposition. Wealthy aristocrats from one thousand years ago didn't have air conditioning. They didn't have modern medical care. They didn't have on-demand access to foods from around the world. They had no Internet, movies, or TV shows. They didn't even have electricity. The average American has access to all of those things; many low-income Americans do.

What those aristocrats did have was *more*. More than almost everyone else. They were at the top of the socioeconomic hierarchy of their time. The average American has more luxuries, with the exception of housing, than the aristocrats of old. However, being in the middle or lower end of the socioeconomic hierarchy of our time doesn't feel very good. To illustrate this, let's learn from the story of Jacob, a five-year-old who likes chocolate.

Jacob's parents open a bag of chocolates and ask him how many pieces he wants. He answers, "Three." They give him three pieces, and he's happy. Next, his siblings ask for three pieces as well. Unfortunately, there weren't enough left in the bag, so they were only given one each. Now his siblings are jealous, and Jacob is even happier due to his good fortune.

A few minutes later, their parents open a new bag of chocolates, and give each of his siblings five more pieces. Now each of his siblings has six pieces, Jacob has three, and the last bag of chocolates is empty. Since Jacob only has half the chocolate of his siblings, he complains that life is unfair, and it ruins the rest of his day.

When Jacob had the most chocolate, he was in great spirits.

When he had the least chocolate, he felt as if he had been cheated. His emotional state changed significantly based on what happened to others, despite having received what he originally asked for. Ironically, he was happier before he had any chocolate than he was when he had three pieces and his siblings had six. Having none felt better than having the least.

The question isn't always, "What is my life like?" It's often, "How good is my life compared to theirs?" whoever "theirs" is referring to. The term "good" only makes sense in comparison to something worse. Benchwarmers in the NBA are phenomenal basketball players compared to practically all of us. Compared to Michael Jordan, they don't seem good at all. Are they good or bad at basketball? It's your choice.

Comparing ourselves to each other and then being content or upset about our relative position is part of human nature. Unfortunately, it's not going anywhere. When this process brings us down, thinking objectively instead of relativistically often paints a brighter picture.

Many politicians, religious leaders, content creators, and other shapers of political discourse can be considered ideologues. Ideologues often compare our society to hypothetical better societies that they imagine. This isn't always a bad thing. Dr. Martin Luther King Jr.'s "I Have a Dream" speech was an invitation to the hypothetical world he dreamed into existence. We have to be able to imagine better possibilities and then pursue them. That's how we make progress. However, we should take care to remain grounded in reality.

If you look at the world and search for everything wrong with it, imagining all the hypothetical ways it could be better, there may be no end to the pessimism that follows.

- Why is traffic so bad in my city?
- Why can't humans live much longer than a century?
- Why do we have parasites and diseases?
- Why is the minimum wage so low?
- Inflation is too high.
- College should be cheaper.
- We need more Blacks and Hispanics in top universities.
- Stop Asian hate.
- Black lives matter.
- All lives matter.

The list never ends. Many of the above issues are real, relevant, and worth discussion. Still, if all we see when we look at the world are problems like these, it becomes a dark place. You want to see real darkness? Zoom out. Keep zooming out until you see a little blue marble, earth. Everything else in the picture, besides the little blue marble of hope, is an uninhabitable death machine. This is it. Earth is precious. It's not perfect, but while we're zoomed out looking at the rest of the bleak universe, who are we to demand perfection?

It sounds funny to say it, but thinking objectively can be a spiritual experience. It's a skill that scientists are usually pretty good at. The scientist's job is to expand our understanding using the tools of repeatable experiments and statistics. These are objective activities based on real things that happened in the past.

Because of their work, scientists often juxtapose our circumstance not against slices of imaginary utopias like ideologues, but against other real circumstances in history. This perspective often leads to a deep appreciation of the current moment that some would describe as spiritual. On the subject of spirituality, the late astronomer and science educator Dr. Carl Sagan remarked, "Science is not only compatible with spirituality; it is a profound source of spirituality."

Based on our best estimates, humans in our current form, *Homo sapiens*, have been on earth for approximately three hundred thousand years. Most of that time was brutal. A nomadic hunter-gatherer might-makes-right free-for-all. We didn't have institutions to protect us. Slavery and sex crimes were rampant. No one had any "rights," and women had fewer than that. Hundreds of thousands of years of high infant mortality rates, starvation, freezing, tribal warfare, etc. None of the religions of today existed. We didn't even have writing technology like paper and printing to pass knowledge into the future. It was generation upon generation of suffering, with little progress to show for it.

How many of our ancestors would trade places with us, exchanging their problems for our problems? Remind me what our problems are again? Affirmative action and figuring out who goes to which bathrooms? Juxtaposition.

The purpose of this line of inquiry isn't to become complacent because the past was worse than the present. It's to take a moment to appreciate our good fortune. To varying degrees, we're all winners in the lottery of life. Not only due to the timing of our births. Due to the fact that our father's one in one hundred million sperm reached our mother's one in one hundred thousand egg. That we are blessed with the human experience at all. Most other animals have only a fraction of our intelligence and lifespan. Like the earth, our lives aren't perfect, but they are precious.

Now that we've taken time to count our blessings, I'll admit that we do have real, serious problems. When Sagan wasn't enlightening the public on the virtues of science, he was warning our leaders about the dangers of nuclear war. In the height of the Cold War, when nuclear risk was at its peak, Sagan worked to inform leaders of the United States and the Soviet Union about the consequences of a nuclear winter. About the truth that a nuclear war cannot be won, and therefore must not be fought. In a 1988 meeting with President Reagan, Soviet leader Mikhail Gorbachev noted that Sagan was a major influence on ending nuclear proliferation.

Sagan, the spiritual scientist, fought to protect the blue marble. The only force powerful enough to damage Mother Earth besides nature herself, is us.

2. Bring the Light

"Darkness cannot drive out darkness — only light can do that."
– Dr. Martin Luther King Jr.

♪ *Nine in the Afternoon* | Panic! at the Disco

It's nearly impossible to establish good faith in a fistfight. Even in a shouting match, the chances are slim. Dark environments are simply not conducive to coming together in a positive, mutually beneficial way. Unfortunately, darkness blankets the landscape of modern political discourse. It's up to us to bring the light.

Establishing good faith after sharing a laugh with someone isn't a tall order. Even so-called tough guys probably aren't looking for conflict on Christmas morning. Statistically speaking, it's rarely Christmas, and we can't always rely on our good humor to set the scene. So, how can we reliably brighten dark situations to maximize our chances of establishing good faith? Be stubbornly positive, and focus on the future.

Conversations about the past tend to be messy. People find reasons to blame others for what happened. We often have incorrect or incomplete facts. Furthermore, we can be overconfident, making unverifiable assertions about how things would have turned out had a different decision been made. It's easy to complain about the current circumstance; it's difficult to predict alternate courses of history given the power of the butterfly effect. Most importantly, the past isn't going to change. Productivity only exists in relation to the future, where we still have the power to make a positive difference. It's good to learn from the past, but we're learning in order to use what we've learned sometime in the future.

Stubborn positivity doesn't mean accepting disrespect and being happy about it. It means giving people the benefit of the doubt. Maintaining a respectful composure even as someone is trying to goad you into a conflict. Being friendly. Having patience. You don't need to do all of these things all of the time. We're not robots with limitless poise and optimism. Just keep the phrase "stubbornly positive" in mind the next time you need to conjure a little light. Then guide the conversation toward the future.

Good Afternoon

"Good afternoon," and then it was over. Mission accomplished. It wasn't easy to say those two words, but I believe you can do it too, if you try. Indeed, I'm quite proud of myself. To the untrained eye it may look like a common greeting. It is, but it was also a spell. A spell to be admired by the likes of Harry Potter himself. A spell that successfully disarmed my enemy and turned her into an ally.

It was the summer of 2020, and I had just moved into the neighborhood. I was renting, and the previous tenant hadn't maintained the yard very well. I decided to make a day of it, and got to work. It was a long day. Most of my time was spent manually cutting and gathering thick treelike vines that were growing into the chain-link fence.

At the end I was exhausted, with a large pile of vines on the ground before me. "Almost done, where should I put them?" I thought to myself. The best idea I had at the time was to deposit them in a dumpster in the alley behind the property. I was aware that it would take up a lot of space in a public dumpster, but there were many others in the alley, so that's what I decided to do.

As I'm putting some vines into the dumpster, I'm alerted that I have a new opponent. I turn to my right to find an angry middle-aged White woman charging toward me about forty feet away. A dangerous specimen, and primed for battle.

Her body language was aggressive; she was shaking her head and screaming negativity at me, the precise words I don't recall. My first instinct was to mirror her hostility and demand respect. You don't just stomp up to me screaming and making demands. Who do you think you are, and more importantly, who do you think I am? I wanted to disrespect her in retaliation for her disrespecting me. To dominate her into submission for daring to start a conflict with me.

That's what I wanted to do. What I did, was put on a smile and say, "Good afternoon." At first she didn't hear me because she was still busy screaming at me.

She paused, then asked, "What did you say?"

Still smiling—"Good afternoon."

She was stumped. "Good afternoon," she said skeptically. "Do you know you're not supposed to put yard waste in there?"

"Where should I put it?"

Now she was on my side. She told me where to buy bags for yard waste, when and where the truck comes to pick them up, asked if I wanted some of her bags, and even offered to help me clean up everything. With a little good faith, she went from enemy to employee in less than two minutes. I declined her offer to work with me as I wasn't keen to continue interacting with her, but I was happy to end the day with a new friend in the neighborhood instead of an enemy. I don't know for sure, but I'd bet she felt the same way.

I could have chosen to amplify her negativity back to her. Instead, I chose the more difficult option—peace. Why? *Selfishly*, I'd rather not have an angry Karen in the neighborhood looking for opportunities to make my life worse. She could have made up some reason to call the police. How would I look as an angry Black man in a confrontation with a White woman in a back alley? I don't want those problems. I don't think it's likely that police would harm me without a good reason, but I don't want to have many opportunities to test it either. *Practically*, that whole "dominate them with further negativity until they regret challenging you" plan rarely works. It would have likely just escalated into an even uglier state than it started. You have to draw the line somewhere, lest it actually end with violence and, more likely for me than for her, prison.

On their own, the selfish and practical arguments wouldn't have been strong enough to overcome my instinct to tell her off. *Principally*, I didn't want to perpetuate another negative butterfly effect. I accepted her hostile disrespect, transformed it, and gave calm, open-minded respect back to her.

Against my instincts, I chose honor, and I'm glad I did. At the end of the day we're animals, and these instincts are the first ones that appear in our minds. A bear doesn't have the mental capacity to understand honor, let alone embody it. What's our excuse? When our better judgment and honor restrain our instincts is when we become worthy of our intelligence, compared to the other animals of course.

Despite my colorful language, this story is closer to extra ordinary than it is to extraordinary. That makes it better. Sure, I could have shared a more heroic story, but how often does anyone have the opportunity to be heroic? Besides, practically everyone would be the hero if they could. How many would choose to respond with positivity and respect after being met with the opposite?

Saying "good afternoon" to your angry neighbor doesn't seem like much, but that small injection of light seeds the beginning of a positive butterfly effect. A single individual can have armies of positive butterflies spread across the world, acting as antibodies against the disease of tribalism. Most of the value is generated passively over time, but it requires an investment in good faith to get the process started.

I'm a Box

It's paramount to establish good faith. Bringing the light is a good way to make your conversation partner receptive to it. However, sometimes we lose the appetite for good faith ourselves. Suppose someone just said that your perspective is one of the dumbest things they've ever heard. Pure idiocy. Good faith is less appealing now, isn't it? This is our test, remaining stubbornly positive in spite of negative remarks.

Decoupling the person from their beliefs makes it easier to pass this test. Imagine people are boxes containing ideas represented by slips of paper. The goal is to remove the bad slips of paper from the box, not throw away the entire box.

You may think that an idea a person has is stupid or immoral; it very well could be both. This, however, doesn't mean that the person is stupid or immoral. The person is a box. Respect the box. If you remove the bad ideas from the box, the box becomes a person worthy of your respect. This wonderful transformation can only happen if you choose to respect the box (person) in the first place, despite its bad ideas.

There is a TED talk where a man named Aaron Stark shares the story of how he nearly became a school shooter. As a child, he grew up in poverty with violent, drug-addicted parents. He was always the new kid in school since his parents never stayed in one place very long. They moved multiple times per year. This made it difficult for him to make friends, which wasn't helped by the fact that he smelled bad since he rarely had showers or clean clothes. He was overweight and a bit socially awkward.

Due to the misfortune of being born into the wrong situation, he was frequently met with new bullies every time he changed schools. They shot him with toy harpoons, joking that he was fat like a whale. They threw food at him, and more. Home was no escape. His own family frequently berated him as well, calling him worthless.

This social torment slowly built up a darkness inside of him that gave him some comfort. Darkness being "comforting" may not make sense to people who haven't been there before, but there is a peace and simplicity to it. Accepting the darkness instead of fighting it. It's a way of giving up. He embraced it. He figured that "there are good people and there are bad people. I must be one of the bad people."

By the age of fifteen, his parents had kicked him out and he was homeless; he didn't want to be around their constant drunken fighting anyway. Living on the streets, he began stealing from his friends and lying, continuing to embrace the dark identity he had assumed.

Aaron did have a friend who stuck by his side despite the fact that he had stolen from him and lied to him too. Aaron slept in his friend's family's dirty shed. One evening lying in that dark shed, rain leaking onto him and blood dripping from his arm from self-inflicted cuts, he realized he would likely soon end up killing himself. Faced with his own mortality, he made an effort to improve his life by calling social services to get professional help.

Unfortunately, when he met with social services, they also brought his mother in. She was one of his biggest sources of pain. His mother managed to persuade the social workers that he was lying, making things up because he wanted attention. They sent him home with her and she said, "Next time you should do a better job and I'll buy you the razor blades." Brutal, coming from his own mother. He had hit rock bottom, called out for help, and then gotten crushed again by the woman who brought him into the world.

Where do you go from there? Further back into that comforting darkness of course. He no longer had anything to lose; any hope for a more positive future was gone. Anger filled the void where the hope he had used to be. He bought a gun from his parent's drug dealer. His goal was to find a place to do "the largest amount of damage in the shortest amount of time, with the least amount of security." He planned to conduct his attack at either a school or a mall food court.

Fortunately, the attack he had planned never happened. The lives of all of his potential victims, as well as the life of Aaron himself, were saved by the friend whose shed he was sleeping in. This friend was the only one who brought light into Aaron's dark life. He saw Aaron was in a bad place mentally, and wanted to help.

He didn't sit him down and say, "Hey, you look like you're in trouble. Is there anything I can do for you?" He simply asked Aaron if he wanted to get something to eat, and maybe watch a movie. In Aaron's words, just, "Treated it like it was a Tuesday. Treated me like I was a person. When someone treats you like a person when you don't even feel like a human, it will change your entire world."

In the TED talk, Aaron expressed his concern that the increase in school shootings would cause people to further distrust and alienate kids like he used to be. "Instead of looking at that kid like he's a threat, look at him like he might be a friend," Aaron asked the TED audience. Today, Aaron is a family man with a wife and four children. He's still friends with the guy who saved his life by showing a little positivity—a kind, human connection. Aaron's call to action at the end of his talk was to "give love to those we think deserve it the least, because they need it the most."

Quite a moving story, I encourage you to look it up and watch the TED talk yourself if you want to hear it in his own voice. Upon concluding his talk, he had won the hearts of the crowd, receiving a standing ovation. This is great, but let's not forget that this man was one movie night away from being added to the long list of school shooters who have our collective scorn. One slice of pizza away from putting tens of innocent people six feet into the ground. He very easily could be rotting in prison right now, with some of the same people applauding him wishing the death sentence upon him.

Why must I ruin a happy ending with such negative thoughts? Because I want to make the point that Aaron Stark, like me, is a box. This box started mostly empty like all boxes do as an innocent child. Over time, as it was beaten and battered by life, slips of paper with dark and evil ideas found their way into the box. Eventually the box included a plan for a mass shooting.

At this point, when Aaron was angry and filled with murderous intent, could you blame someone who knew about his plans for hating him? For using any means necessary to stop him from killing innocent people? In the state of mind he was in at that moment, he was a school shooter, he just hadn't done it yet.

In this situation we have the benefit of knowing his backstory, but most of the time we don't. Because of this, it is best to lead with understanding. You never know what people have gone through to end up where they are. This doesn't mean that it's OK to be where they are, but rather to hold off on being too personal with your judgments; step off the high horse for a bit.

A soon-to-be school shooter is planning his attack. What should we do? Imprison him before he can shoot up the school? Use lethal force? No need, his friend brought a little light. He showed kindness to someone who was in that moment among the worst of us, a school shooter. He showed kindness to a school shooter, and because of that, he was no longer a school shooter. He respected the box, and then the box became worthy of respect. Worthy of a standing ovation. Not Aaron, his friend who brought the light.

We the People

The increasingly polarized political environment causes each election to feel more important than the last. As tribalism grows, the consequences of the other side winning grow with it. From a liberal perspective, part of this phenomenon can be attributed to how uniquely bad Trump is. However, Trumpism is a part of the Republican Party now, and will likely remain so for the foreseeable future.

Traditional conservative leadership doesn't like having to deal with Trumpism for two reasons. The first reason is ideological; they don't like some of Trump's policy positions, and how he's redefining the GOP. The second reason for their discontent is practical; Trumpism can be unnecessarily divisive, which contributes to them losing winnable races.

In the 2022 midterms, far-right election-denying candidates supported by Trump significantly underperformed expectations, crushing the GOP's hopes for a "red wave." At the same time, Republican Governor Ron DeSantis accomplished another great electoral victory in Florida. The GOP establishment, like all wealthy investors, wanted to put money behind something that was winning.

Just like Trump's run in 2016, what the investors want doesn't matter. It's about what the market wants. Even if the GOP establishment leadership wants to minimize the MAGA impact on elections, they have no choice but to deal with it as long as it remains a significant portion of the Republican base.

Though I'm saddened by Trump's ability to convince many Republican voters that he actually cares about them or the country, I'm happy that it indicates our democracy is still working. My conspiracy-minded friends on both sides of the aisle surprise me with how powerful they think the elite are.

The "deep state" billionaire establishment runs everything? If that's the case, why did Trump win the Republican nomination? If the Clintons are so powerful, why did Hillary lose every time she tried to run for president? She lost to a far less establishment candidate in 2008 named Barack Hussein Obama. She then lost to one of the least establishment candidates of all time named Donald Trump. The Republican's supervillain George Soros failed to keep Trump from the Oval Office.

The "deep state" is looking more like the "weak state" if you ask me. Democracy worked. It isn't a perfect form of government. Sometimes we choose to elect someone like Trump. The benefit of democracy is that we're only stuck with Trump for four years, not for life, followed by his children. My conservative friends probably wouldn't look forward to a Hunter Biden presidency either.

If the "establishment" is Goliath, then we, the people, are David. This is the story of America. Don't let fearmongering media make you feel powerless. Quite the contrary. I think they're afraid of us. I smell weakness. What do you call it when the GOP establishment that couldn't stand Trump supported him once they realized they couldn't beat him? What do you call it when politicians "evolve" their political views based on what's popular in the current moment? Pandering for public support? Certainly not strength. We the people wield the power, so long as this country remains a democracy.

The leaders in both parties can't move without our support. Therefore, I don't think it matters much who the leaders are. It matters who we are. Our leaders reflect us, not vice versa. This polarized political environment isn't Trump's fault or Biden's fault. It's not the Clintons' or the Bushes' fault. It's our fault, regular people. This is good, because it means we have the power to fix it.

Divided We Fall

"Leading with positivity and understanding so we can come together is nice, but why do that when we can win? Wouldn't it be better if we simply defeated Republicans instead?" – Susan

I want Democrats to win elections too, Susan. I'm not some neutral parent-like figure asking the kids to play nice. I have a horse in the race, and I have biases like practically everyone else. With that said, I'd like to share some wisdom from my late great-grandmother. She told us, "You catch more flies with honey than you do with vinegar."

In what context was she trying to catch flies? I have no idea, but I think the aphorism applies in this case. I believe we'll have more success at the ballot box by simply injecting a little light and good faith into our interactions with conservatives. This doesn't require a shift to the center on matters of policy; I think this will be a more successful strategy even if our policy positions stay the same. We'll have more success in elections and be reducing tribalism at the same time. Win-win.

At the heart of Susan's question lies two options. Either we come together in good faith with our Republican friends or we resolve to fight them better. The United States of America, or the Divided States of America. Our geopolitical competitors like China and Russia prefer the latter. Americans continuing to divide. Tribalism pitting us against each other. Losing faith in our institutions. Losing standing with our allies when we break our agreements between administrations. Our competitors don't just want to divide the US from within; they want to weaken our international alliances, break up NATO, and break up the EU.

As they're trying to convince us to be smaller, and step down from the world stage, they're doing the opposite. Russia has been trying to take Ukraine by force. China has its eye on removing the ambiguity around Taiwan. The BRICS nations are coming together to attempt to rival the power of the dollar and the euro. At the same time, they try to sell us our demise under the guise of "America first." I hope we're not so foolish. Our competitors are grouping up against us. They're trying to sow discord between us and our allies to get us to split up. Let's not take the bait.

Foreign policy is about relationships. Understanding leaders, their culture, and motivations. With your allies, it's about friendship. Friendship not just based on emotion and having a shared culture, but long-term interest alignment. Commitment to having each other's backs, being reliable, and so on.

Conservative commentator Candace Owens was a guest speaker on the *PBD Podcast* where she said, "F Ukraine ... not just Ukraine, F everybody until we get our house in order." This is a common conservative perspective—"F everybody, America first." What kind of friend does that sound like? Not one I'd trust or want to work with. Then, and I found this funny, she went on to discuss the value of diplomacy.

Her diplomatic approach is essentially, "F all of you, I only care about myself. Now let's work together." The fundamentals of human decency don't go away just because you're in government. This attitude is not that of a good friend. You don't want to hear this sentiment from your allies. It's the attitude of someone you can only rely on to act in their self-interest. With friends like that, who needs enemies? Even if you are solely self-interested, people seem to have a hard time understanding that it's in our interest to have friends.

The fundamentals are quite simple. There is strength in numbers. Suppose Greg trains hard, eventually becoming skilled enough to defeat the mixed martial arts heavyweight champion of the world. Most people would agree that Greg is quite powerful. If Brandon is skilled enough to organize twenty guys and find Greg alone, Brandon is more powerful.

Power, in military and economic contexts, is about scale. Being alone is near synonymous with being weak. Weakness invites aggression from those who stand to benefit from it. We want to be strong, but where does strength come from? Some of it comes from our military, and our economy. Most of it comes from the militaries and economies of our allies. Becoming world champion is impressive, but remember—Greg loses to Brandon.

Can our competitors outmuscle Italy alone in global power politics and economics? Yes. How about the EU together? That's much tougher. Add in the United States and other friendly nations, including but not limited to Canada, Australia, Japan, and Israel, and they have little chance. An outright military attack would end horribly for everyone but if we lose, they'd lose more. However, poison us from within and get us to turn on each other, to fight ourselves? They could win the war with media alone and never need to fire a shot. They can't beat us, but tribalism can.

Unfortunately, our global competitors find willing partners for their agenda in modern conservative political leaders. Not just media commentators and influencers, but people with decision-making power within our governments. Some MAGA Republicans like Marjorie Taylor Green speak as fondly of a "national divorce" as President Putin or Xi would.

At rallies, some of their constituents sport shirts saying, "I'd rather be a Russian than a Democrat." Take note fellow liberals, this means they like and/or trust a foreign country we're in conflict with more than us. This makes them look unpatriotic, but it makes us look bad too. They abhor us so much they'd rather turn to Russia? Putin would be proud. We as Americans should be ashamed. Sure, it's on the right side of the aisle, but it should cause us to look in the mirror to understand why they feel that way.

America should be a bastion of light, leading by example to show the world what a functioning democracy by the people, for the people looks like. A country with friends and strong alliances across the world. A place where no one is above the law, and there is minimal corruption. Our competitors don't want to see this America.

They want us to doubt ourselves. To think we're just as corrupt as many of them are. For pessimism to become synonymous with wisdom. To hate and destroy each other. Whoever wins, they win. We can't let this happen. We can't take the bait.

We need to do the hard thing and extend a friendly hand to those Republicans wearing the "I'd rather be a Russian than a Democrat" shirt. Show them that we're not too bad and they may stop wearing the shirt. Then, maybe we'll learn that they're not too bad either.

I intentionally called Russia, China, and other countries generally opposed to the success of the West "competitors" instead of "enemies." I think it's unwise to call a whole country full of mostly good people working to make ends meet for their families like we are "enemies." I wish nothing but success for everyone; this includes Chinese people, Russian people, Arab people, etc. When we oppose the military aggression of Vladimir Putin, it doesn't mean all Russians are our enemies. We need to stand against the aggression, but the aggression is the enemy, not "Russians."

Our competitors want to sell the story that "the evil West is out to get them." We are powerful, and we're not their allies, so I can understand their people having a predisposition against us. Imagine you're camping and a bear roams your campground. The bear isn't showing you any aggression, but you'll still probably build a plan to defend yourself against it. Even if you're not going to attack the bear, you may want to find a way to weaken it. We're the bear. It's not bad to be the bear, but we don't have to go around growling at people, motivating them to further conspire against us. As President Theodore Roosevelt used to say, speak softly and carry a big bear … or something like that.

I implore you not to get sucked into the endless cycle of negativity and pessimism. Tribalism feeds on pessimism. They have bad intentions for us, so we respond with bad intentions for them, and no one remembers who started it. They want to drink leftist tears? They'd rather be a Russian than a Democrat? Extend a friendly hand anyway. Trying to reach a common understanding with the other side of the aisle doesn't make you a traitor; in these polarized times, it makes you a patriot.

Like my interaction with the angry woman in the alley, if we choose to escalate, we have to draw the line somewhere, lest it end in violence. Conservatives aren't going anywhere, and despite our best efforts, we're not going to win every election. When we lose, I'd rather see a John McCain-like Republican in office, rest in peace, than a Trumpian one.

We're regular people. We have jobs to do and families to care for. We don't have to set out to change the world, but we can bring a little light with us. If we can express sympathy and understanding for Aaron Stark, the would-be school shooter, we can do the same for supporters of Marjorie Taylor Green.

"*Good afternoon.*"

"*Wanna watch a movie?*"

A little light can brighten a lot of darkness.

3. Check Your Bias

"A person's life persuades better than his word."
— Aristotle

♫ The Preacher | Bing Crosby & Louis Armstrong

Understanding and good faith. These are the two ingredients necessary for reducing tribalism. Bias tends to make us less interested in understanding each other. If we strongly believe that we're right and our opponents are wrong, why would we try to understand something that's wrong?

"We don't need to understand them, they need to understand us" is a common perspective that keeps us talking past each other. Both sides often share the overconfidence that their current perspective is the best possible perspective. Real confidence is listening with an open mind to the other side, and being willing to change your mind when they make good arguments.

I recently read a book on persuasion called *Thank You for Arguing* by Jay Heinrichs. In his book, Heinrichs outlined three types of argument.

Logos: Argument by logic
Ethos: Argument by character
Pathos: Argument by emotion

I was quite upset to learn that among the three types of argument, my favorite, *logos*, is usually the least effective. I still maintain a dream of living in a fairy-tale land where *logos* reigns supreme and no one is distracted by *ethos* or *pathos*. A dream where your ideas are judged not by mood of the audience, or by the content of your character, but by the quality of your logic. The previous statement itself is an *ethos* appeal, building trust with those who consider themselves intellectuals. Which, given that you're reading a book like this, you likely are. Yet again, another *ethos* appeal, as I've implied that we're both members of the unfortunately small "intellectual" tribe. This is horrible, isn't it?

It begs the question, if we're not making decisions using logic, what are we using? Emotion and character? An unsettling prospect. Even if we're not using logic, hopefully we're smart enough to know that we *should* be using it. The example below demonstrates just how weak *logos* is. The goal is to get the student to go to the library and study.

Logos:
Teacher: "After class, go to the library and study because being educated is best for your happiness in the long run."
Student: "No."

Pathos:
Attractive classmate: "Want to come study with me in the library?"
Student: "Sure!"

Ethos:
Father: "Go to the library and study, I'll pick you up at six."
Student: "Yes, sir."

This is an abomination. I'm ashamed to be human, but the truth is the truth.

Preaching to the Choir

Though *logos* fell short of my expectations, *ethos* surprised me. I believe that *ethos* is the most powerful type of argument by far. *Ethos* has the magical power of making us inclined to agree. Negative *ethos* can even make us inclined to disagree. This biased mental state of being *inclined* to agree or disagree with someone is more effective than almost any logical argument. Poor *ethos* almost guarantees failure in persuasion.

Suppose Ezekiel has plans to address a Black church on Sunday morning. Ezekiel is a guest preacher with a good reputation. He's also Black, and he's wearing a nice suit with a fresh haircut, so he has good decorum. He walks up to the podium and begins a traditional call and response for this community.

Ezekiel: "God is good!"
Audience: "All the time."
Ezekiel: "And all the time?"
Audience: "God is good!"
Ezekiel: "Amen."
Audience: "Amen."

Ethos check passed. The audience is now receptive to whatever Ezekiel has to say, "amen" locked and loaded on their tongues. This doesn't mean they will concur with literally anything he says next, but it's a friendly audience and maintaining their support should be a layup.

Imagine it's the same Black church on Sunday morning but with a different guest speaker this time, Sawyer. Sawyer is an unkempt White man with disheveled, balding hair, poorly cloaked by a red "Make America Great Again" hat. Sawyer has a reputation for being a racist. It doesn't matter what this man says, he already lost. Sawyer could be about to share deep wisdom, maximum *logos*. The audience doesn't want to hear it. They physically may not be able to hear him over the boos. He could even try, "God is good!" and they'll just scream at him to get off the stage.

Ezekiel could make a poor logical argument and still get the default agreement the audience had prepared for him due to his impeccable *ethos*. Sawyer could make a perfectly sound logical argument that no one in the audience would give credence to because of his poor *ethos*. Being inclined to agree or disagree with someone is a bad thing if you care about the truth.

Should you not learn anything from a criminal? A child? A racist? A person less intelligent than you? An enemy combatant? Worst of all, a conservative? I'll learn from all of them. It shouldn't matter if the person is good; it only matters if the idea itself is good. This is why I never respected the "you're a hypocrite" attack. If a drug dealer tells kids they shouldn't deal drugs, is he a hypocrite? Yes. Is it good advice? Also, yes.

It was either Greek philosopher Aristotle himself or one of his contemporaries who is quoted as saying, "A person's life persuades better than his word." Due to the strength of *ethos*, I believe this is true, but it's rarely a good thing.

The only arguments for which a person's life is relevant are claims about the individual herself. For example, if Sarah frequently lies to get out of trouble, you may be wise to be skeptical of her words when she's in a precarious situation. If Sarah has been the MVP of her basketball team for two years straight, that's relevant information for deciding whether or not to pass her the ball in a crucial moment. However, being "mean" doesn't make her less likely to be correct about the quadratic formula. It does make us less inclined to agree with her though. This is where *ethos* distracts us from *logos*.

Assuming we do care about truth, we should look to identify situations where we have been influenced by anything other than objective logic. It's not just church where *ethos* bias can impact our beliefs. Most tribal identities can. Example tribes could be your family, ethnicity, gender, political party, faith, nationality, even your species. These tribes often come with some biases or *default* beliefs that you're *supposed* to have as a member of that tribe. These default beliefs aren't necessarily wrong; it just means you should intentionally question them, assuming you haven't been critical of them before.

Political tribalism provides a double dose of *ethos* bias. Positive *ethos* from generally liking the people on your side of the aisle. Negative *ethos* from disliking the opposition. Simply put, you have people you do like arguing against people you don't like. How many of us would side with people we don't like when they're right logically, at the cost of our standing within our own tribe? At the cost of feeling like traitors ourselves? At the cost of giving the other side a victory by showing weakness? Not enough of us.

It's uncomfortable when people you don't like are right, so we often choose to ignore it. To put our minds off of it and go back to the comforting, wishful thinking belief that we're the good guys. That we're protecting the world from our less intelligent, less moral enemies. Abstractly this seems foolish, but in practice, agreeing with people we don't like and are actively opposing is hard to do. It requires discipline, humility, and honesty. Honesty with others, but more importantly, honesty with ourselves.

Intellectual Humility

As mentioned above, it takes discipline, honesty, and humility to keep our biases in check in pursuit of the truth. I've had to do some work internally to improve at this myself. I'm often praised, but I'm not often praised for my humility. During my freshman year of college, I took a philosophy course taught by a professor at the end of his career. The professor's delivery was quite dry, especially for an early morning class. Despite a presentation that had some of my peers dozing off, I found the content we covered quite interesting. It was my favorite class.

The professor and I used to go back and forth in emails discussing and sometimes debating philosophy concepts. During one of these exchanges, he told me I was among the most intelligent students he ever taught. Coming from an old philosophy professor on his way to retirement, I appreciated the compliment. The important part of the story comes next, when he followed his compliment with "but." "But," he said, "you look at ideas you disagree with as concepts to be shot down instead of as opportunities to improve your perspective."

He was right. Most of my energy was spent trying to find and expose everything wrong with what my conversation partner was telling me so I could make them see things my "right" way. I was trying to enhance *their* perspective. In his criticism of me, he was urging me to look for truth even in flawed ideas, to enhance my own. Suggesting that if I did, I'd improve at a faster rate and become even better than I already was at the time. This is the handiwork of a great teacher; I thank him for sharing his wisdom with me. With us.

I still enjoy a friendly verbal sparring session. However, his advice stays with me. I try to consciously incorporate it when I find myself faced with something significant that I disagree with. The *strawman* is a dirty argument tactic where your opponent sets up a weak version of your argument, the "strawman," and then destroys it. For instance, imagine someone is arguing that the legal drinking age should be eighteen instead of twenty-one. Their opponent argues, "We shouldn't let young children do all kinds of drugs," as a response. This is a strawman, arguing against "young children" doing "all kinds of drugs" instead of eighteen-year-old young adults specifically drinking alcohol.

Heeding the advice of my professor, I do the opposite of strawman. I set up a *steelman*, which is the best version of my opponent's argument I can think of. Then, instead of trying to beat the steelman, I sincerely look to find truth or wisdom from it. Sometimes there is none. More often, somewhere in the pile of garbage that is my opponent's argument, there will be a nugget of truth. I appreciate it, pick it up, and I'm better off for having done this exercise.

We all have limited time, so I can understand not questioning every belief you currently hold this way. But when you are taking the time to think, I recommend that you try this process. The hardest part is being sincere when setting up and looking for truth in the steelman. We are obviously biased to agree with our own arguments. Seeking wisdom from the steelman requires you to behave as if you have a bias toward your opponent's argument instead. This exercise is like channeling your inner judge instead of your inner lawyer. "His lawyer agrees with him." Well of course. It's difficult to channel your inner judge when you only actively work on one side of the dispute.

It reminds me of when my parents asked me to help cook fish for dinner as a child. I don't like the taste of fish, but it just so happened to taste better when I helped cook it. I don't think it did really, but the fact that I had some ownership biased me in favor of liking it more. After working on both sides of the dispute, first on your default side, and then on the steelman's side, you're now prepared to attempt to drop the bias from both sides and determine what the best perspective is. In my experience, it's usually mostly my previous perspective, but modified by whatever nuggets of truth I found from the steelman.

When engaging in substantive argument with conservatives, success looks like moving them slightly to the left of where they were or, even better, helping them dislike us a little less. If we lead by example showing some intellectual humility and willingness to change ourselves, there is a better chance of them following suit. This is a good bet to make if you're confident the judge will rule in your favor.

Mighty Convenience

Wanting something to be true is persuasive. I call this the wishful thinking bias. Arguments that are in harmony with your self-interest tend to be highly persuasive as well. Self-interest is the only thing I'd bet on being more powerful than *ethos*. That's why it's so important to get incentives right. It's why capitalism works so well; it assumes we're self-interested, greedy, and not much else. It's not often wrong.

Yes, fellow liberals, we should be proud supporters of capitalism; it's not a "bad word." A mostly free market with sensible regulations to protect people and the environment is the best economic system I've seen implemented. I know conservatives like capitalism and by default we're inclined to disagree with them, but remember, we're both Americans. Besides, if a conservative liked your dog, would it cause you to want to get rid of it?

I believe conservatives do the same in relation to us. We want to protect the environment from climate change. This means conservatives can't believe climate change is really happening, or at the very least it must not be our fault, right? This is a good time to check our biases, steelman the opposing argument and look for some nuggets of truth.

Back on the topic of self-interest, US Vice President Al Gore quoted the author and political activist Upton Sinclair saying, "It is difficult to get a man to understand something, when his salary depends on his not understanding it." Gore was referring to his struggles discussing climate change with business leaders who had an interest in climate change not being real.

In his movie *An Inconvenient Truth*, Gore shares the story of how his father ended up reversing his position on growing tobacco. His father had always been a tobacco farmer. His older sister started smoking cigarettes as a teenager. They knew cigarettes caused cancer, but they kept producing tobacco anyway. Gore's sister eventually got lung cancer and passed away from the very product her family produced. After that, Gore's father couldn't bring himself to keep growing tobacco. He said, "Whatever explanation that had seemed to make sense in the past just didn't cut it anymore."

It's one thing to know factually that you're producing a product that kills people. It's another thing entirely to watch your own daughter struggle and pass away from it. Gore's father and other tobacco farmers aren't immoral or unintelligent. This is a typical human process—not really appreciating the weight of an issue until it affects you or someone you love personally.

It's not hard to find ways to justify it. If the individual farmer stops growing tobacco, smokers will just buy it from someone else. You're not actually saving anyone; you're just making yourself feel better since you're no longer contributing to the problem. The same could be said for dealing other drugs. Add in the self-interest bias of it being costly to end the tobacco business you've already invested in, and there's a good chance that you'll end up choosing to make your money.

Ideally, it shouldn't matter if we personally know someone who died from a drug. It shouldn't matter if a homophobic man personally ends up with a gay brother. If a racist personally has a mixed-race grandchild. If a woman personally raised a cow that was sent for slaughter. It shouldn't matter, but it's often what makes the difference for us flawed humans.

I'm guilty of some cognitive dissonance with the last one. I personally wouldn't kill an animal to eat it, not if I had other options, but I do eat meat. I probably make justifications similar to the ones Gore's father used to make. We should be able to learn without having to personally bump our heads first. To appreciate someone else's experience without having to live it ourselves. I have room to improve in this regard; most of us likely do.

My most memorable experience regarding the power of self-interest happened while pursuing my master's degree in finance. We were required to take a leadership class in order to graduate. Near the end of the semester, the leadership professor told us to bring $5 cash to the next class, and to be prepared to lose it. That's all we knew coming in. We had no idea what kind of exercise we would be doing, or why we needed money for it.

At the beginning of class, he had all of us sit our $5 on the table in front of us. He then walked around the room and spoke to about eight people discreetly. There were approximately forty students in the class. I was not one of the eight students he spoke to. He then told the *Upper Management* to collect all the money.

We sat as three classmates, all Asian women I believe, went around and collected everyone's money. He then said the *Upper Management* knew the objective of this exercise; he wouldn't tell us. He did tell us *Laborers* that we had to leave the classroom, but the *Middle Management* and *Upper Management* could stay. There weren't any unoccupied rooms nearby large enough to seat all of us. We *Laborers* ended up standing uncomfortably in the hallway and partially down the stairway.

No one was upset at this point; we were just curious about the objective of this exercise. Eventually, *Middle Management* was willing to speak with us. To avoid a thirty-person conversation, we *Laborers* decided to send a few representatives. I was chosen as one of the representatives. Another representative was a classmate I'll call John.

We met with *Middle Management* in a small room adjacent to the stairway. We asked what we were supposed to do. They seemed uncertain as well, but there was a rumor that the *Upper Management* was deciding how the money they collected should be distributed in the "company."

Now it was beginning to make sense. We weren't doing anything really. This was an exercise in how to allocate resources with our real money on the line. As the *Laborers* in this exercise with practically no power, it seemed clear we were going to get the short end of the stick. As John and the other representative were reacting to the news, I decided to go out and relay an update to the rest of the *Laborers* still standing in the stairway.

As I was giving my account of the conversation with *Middle Management*, the *Laborers* started to get a bit riled up about the unfairness. About how the management didn't do anything to become management. About the discomfort of being forced to stand in the cramped stairway while less than ten people in the classroom had over fifty comfortable seats. It was then that the professor told me I had been promoted to *Upper Management*.

He brought me into the classroom. When I walked in, I saw *Middle Management* standing together in a group off to the side. The three original members of *Upper Management* were in the center, with approximately $200 in cash in front of them. As I walked up to my fellow members of *Upper Management*, I asked to see the instructions. At this point, I still didn't know for sure what was going on. The instructions were simple; it was our job to allocate the cash among ourselves, *Middle Management*, and the *Laborers*. I believe the *Middle Management's* job was to support *Upper Management*.

I realized we could split the $200 four ways, and go about our business as *Upper Management*. I asked what the plan was. They hadn't yet figured it out, so I said we should give everyone their money back. Though they didn't agree on what to do with the money, they all agreed not to agree with me. I argued on behalf of the *Laborers*: "We don't have any right to keep their money. What if they need it?" And so forth. They wouldn't budge. Since I'm *Upper Management* now and I can do what I want, I decided to go out and address the *Laborers* to give them an update.

As soon as I stepped into the stairway to speak with them, I was met with "boos" from the crowd. Now that I was part of *Upper Management*, their enemy, my *ethos* had turned negative from their perspective. I told them, "Look, I'm your only friend in that room, let me explain what's going on." I proceeded to let them know that I was lobbying on their behalf, but partway through I was told to come back inside by the professor. After a few more minutes of negotiations, me fighting to get the *Laborers* more money, my classmate John walked into the room. Apparently, he was just promoted to *Middle Management*.

Unlike me, John's support of the *Laborers* vanished the moment he walked through the door. He was my fiercest opponent, arguing to give the *Laborers* the bare minimum. It got to the point where I was pulling my *Upper Management* card, arguing that I'd just take a quarter of the money, take my $5 out of it, and then distribute the rest to the *Laborers* on a first-come-first-served basis. Before I could do it the exercise ended. The *Laborers* had revolted and stormed the classroom.

The *Laborers* were asked to take a seat as management remained at the front of the class. The professor guided us through an open debrief of how the exercise felt from different perspectives. He asked how the *Laborers* felt being forced outside and largely kept in the dark. How *Middle Management* felt about *Upper Management*. How *Upper Management* felt about me coming in and shaking things up. Most of the answers were as you'd expect from someone in the position they were in. John's account of his story is what made this so memorable for me.

Initially, John was a *Laborer* like me. After I was promoted to *Upper Management*, he remained outside whipping the *Laborers* up into a frenzy about unfair practices from management. He was a revolutionary fighting for justice. Then he got promoted to *Middle Management*. Without shame, remorse, or embarrassment, he shared how he immediately switched and began lobbying for management to keep the vast majority of the money, leaving the *Laborers* he was leading just two minutes ago with scraps.

I was there, so I knew he didn't want the *Laborers* to have much, but I wasn't aware that moments before he was fervently leading the charge against us. I cringed for him at the optics of having so quickly and shamelessly abandoned his word in favor of his self-interest. He didn't care.

This made me wonder. How many of us are John? Envision a group of one thousand low-income Democrats pushing for an expansion of government social programs to help the poor. These people are supporters of the meek, of those facing adversity, of the underdogs in society. How many of them would turn Republican if they got promoted to *Middle Management* and moved up a few tax brackets? How many of the people pushing for an increase in the minimum wage would still push for it if they were a business owner paying it instead of an employee earning it?

The answer is that some are principled and will remain consistent, and some won't; I don't know the ratio. Until you know someone well enough to have seen their principles take precedence over their self-interest a few times, don't be certain you know who is who. Sometimes even we ourselves aren't as principled as we think we are once a new set of self-interest biases kicks in.

Don't Be a Bot

It's not enough to simply know about types of bias and their tendency to distract us from *logos*. We need to actively look out for these biases in daily life in order to make us less like a "bot." The ultimate "bot" is a person who kept all of the default beliefs from the tribes they were born into. They only incorporate new beliefs into their worldview if those beliefs align with their self-interest, or are ideas they would prefer to be true.

You don't usually even need to talk to a bot. You can guess what the bot is thinking with high accuracy just by knowing their demographic information, socioeconomic status, and a bit about their family. I think of the bot as less like a person, and more like a substance that takes the shape of whatever it's poured into. I mentioned that every "tribe" a person is born into has some *default* beliefs that its members are *supposed* to have. Here are some examples of bot opinions based on the tribe they are poured into.

Human tribe: It's OK to kill, eat, and enslave other animals, but not humans.

Black tribe: Supports affirmative action. Inclined against believing in White supremacy. Open to hearing about reparations for slavery.

White tribe: Against affirmative action. Open to hearing arguments for White supremacy. Inclined against hearing about reparations for slavery.

Christian tribe: Jesus is the best messenger.

Muslim tribe: Mohammed is the best messenger.

Spiritual tribe: Did you get the message?

American tribe: America is exceptional because we're American.

Male tribe: Less inclined to complain about the "patriarchy." More inclined to long for the days when women didn't compete as much with men in the workplace.

Female tribe: Inclined to complain about the "patriarchy." Likely to support the advancement of feminism even after women have gained equality under the law.

Here are some examples of self-interest bots.
- My little boy is an angel, the teachers just need to do a better job.
- My people are discriminated against and need special protections.
- God is on our side in this war.
- The sports team from my area is the best!
- Something bad happened, it must be because of the opposing party's administration.
- Something good happened, it must be because of my party's administration.
- I deserve this promotion more than anyone else!
- Oh no, our team failed! I must figure out who to blame, besides me of course.
- Things would be better if we had more people who looked like me in charge.
- Legislation that will help my people? Great!
- Legislation that will help other people with my tax dollars? This isn't fiscally responsible.

- The 2020 election was stolen from Trump!
- Biden won in 2020 fair and square.

Here is a non-exhaustive list of issues Republicans and Democrats often disagree about.
- Foreign policy
- Fiscal policy (taxes and government spending)
- Monetary policy (managing the money supply and interest rates)
- Environmental policy
- Business regulations
- Abortion
- Christian vs secular values
- LGBTQIA+ in general, and in schools
- Border control and immigration
- Gun regulations
- Electoral College
- Voter fraud
- Masks and vaccines

Not all political issues are on the above list, but the Republican bot has the mainstream Republican position on every issue, and the Democrat bot has the mainstream Democratic position on every issue. I don't mean for this section to come across like I'm saying the bots are always wrong. Sometimes the bots are right. However, when they're right it's from good fortune, not from good thinking. Some folks reading this may share Sam's opinion.

"Hold on there. For every tribe I'm a part of, the default beliefs were right even after objective critical questioning of them. My family

has great values. My faith is the one true faith among all the others that people made up. I don't have any extremist views based on my gender or race. My country is actually exceptional, and my political party happens to have the correct perspective on every issue." — Sam

It is possible for someone to have been born and indoctrinated with all of the best ideas from the start. Though given how many boxes there are to check, this is incredibly unlikely. If you think all of your default beliefs were perfect, realize it's much more likely that you're still holding on to some biases.

However, if you are indeed so lucky as to have had everything right by default, with no need to change your mind about anything; if everything that's in your interest also happens to be the right thing that should be done; if you think these are all objectively the best policies, appreciate the mountain of good fortune that was blessed upon you at your birth. Then, show some understanding for those of us who weren't as fortunate. Some of whom may have been born into tribes with many, or all of the wrong beliefs.

Not only do these tribes make them start off wrong by default. They also come with biases that make it harder for them to become right, even after being met with good evidence and logic. This is why we should have patience and understanding for people.

Most real people aren't entirely bots. Ultimate bots do exist, but they're rare. Most of us still have some incorrect bot beliefs; we just don't know which ones they are. My simple advice is for us to immediately get nervous and cast doubt upon any of the following types of beliefs.

- Beliefs we started with by default that haven't changed
- Beliefs that are in our best interest

- Beliefs that we would prefer to be true

I'll give an uncomfortable real-life example. As a Black man, I'd prefer White supremacy not to be true. This was also, unsurprisingly, the default belief of my family. Following the above guidelines, I realized my bias against White supremacy could have been getting in the way of my *logos* on the topic. All bias is bad if you care about being correct.

With this in mind, I decided to engage with White supremacist individuals and literature with a more open mind than I was comfortable with. At the end of that experience, I still wasn't persuaded in favor of White supremacy. My mind didn't change, but I did give it an honest, unbiased chance.

During that process, I was able to understand how a White person with a self-interest bias and political grievances could find the concept compelling and, with limited critical thinking, become convinced it's actually true. It's certainly more appealing to believe that you're a member of the world's preeminent race engaged in a struggle against elites, than it is to admit you're just a regular guy on the low end of society.

It's not pleasant to take concepts seriously that are the antithesis of our current beliefs or identities. This type of discomfort, however, is what we must endure to occasionally improve our perspectives. This is sometimes the cost of investing in good faith understanding.

Boiled Frog Problems

There are certain types of problems humans are bad at solving. Immediate, urgent, problems usually get taken care of. Gradual, long-term problems are the ones we struggle to address. For example, if we're credibly notified that a terrorist group is going to attack our family in the next couple of weeks, we're going to do something about it today. If instead, we're credibly notified that our family will die from obesity in fifteen years, we're probably not going to do anything about it, and we'll have some funerals to attend halfway through the next decade. We'll regret it in about thirteen years, but by then it will be too late.

Similarly, there is a personalization bias that causes us to make poor logical decisions and trade-offs between issues. If we can put a face to the things harming us, like terrorists or school shooters, we're more likely to have an emotional *pathos* response and take action. However, when disease, weather, aging, obesity, or anything else nonpersonal kills us, it's considered more acceptable. This is the case even when the nonpersonal threat is similarly preventable and harms significantly more people.

Many of us would have a stronger emotional reaction if a terrorist killed one hundred people than if a disease killed ten thousand. If someone were to tell you with certainty that you're going to die in two months, do you care whether it's because of a person or because of a force of nature? Maybe you do, but the difference is largely emotional.

Personally, I'd like to see more people take the aging problem seriously. Every person on earth is born with the disease of aging that will kill them eventually. We're born on death row. We've gotten used to it so we just accept it, but if we can solve it, it's more valuable than almost everything else.

Al Gore uses the boiled frog analogy to describe climate change. If a frog jumps into a pot of boiling water, it will jump out. If instead, it jumps into lukewarm water that is slowly brought to a boil, the frog will remain until it, hopefully, is rescued. To me, tribalism is another one of those "boiled frog" problems. It's not an emergency that needs to be fixed tomorrow. Ironically, many of us who do care about tribalism simply blame the other side for it, believing that it's their responsibility to fix. In the future, we probably won't be able to pinpoint exactly when things went wrong, but we'll wish we had tried to fix it sooner.

The cost of unchecked tribalism isn't just the risk of increased political violence or, worst case, a second civil war. The main cost is gradually making poorer and poorer decisions over time. Tribalism does this by making us identify more as enemies to each other, than as Americans with slightly different solutions to common problems. Identifying as enemies ingrains biases that create a race to the fringes on both sides. This makes any medium- to long-term plan for the nation impossible, since the next administration may move in the opposite direction of the prior one.

How can we bring the world together to solve a problem like climate change if we can't even bring our own country together on the issue? We led the world in the Obama administration to set up the Paris Climate Agreement. Then Donald Trump got elected and we left it. We as a nation look ridiculous. We go through all the fuss about getting everyone to sign up and agree, and then we quit.

Fixing the tribalism problem will improve our decision-making as a nation considerably on almost all issues. It will also improve our credibility on the world stage, strengthening our capacity to lead. It's not as exciting as the war on terror. It doesn't appear to be as consequential as climate change. Yet, it may well be the prerequisite needed to successfully address most of the issues we face.

In *An Inconvenient Truth*, Gore notes that our ancestors could make mistakes without the consequences of them being too long-lasting or extreme. We don't have that privilege. As time goes on and we become more powerful, the consequences of our mistakes become more permanent and dangerous.

We didn't ask for this responsibility, but it is upon us. I believe it is the role of the United States to lead in this important moment. If we disagree with each other just because we don't like each other, and always happen to arrive at the most convenient opinion that serves our short-term interests, how are we going to make good decisions? We need to become better people to become a better country. Our civility needs an upgrade to keep up with our power. This is our burden to bear.

Bertrand Russell was a mathematician and philosopher who passed away at age ninety-seven in 1970. Eleven years before his death, he was asked what his advice would be for future generations. Though Russell passed away before my parents were born, his answer to this question makes me believe we are kindred spirits. It also nearly perfectly summarizes where we're at in the book so far. I'll let Russell's wisdom close the chapter.

> Interviewer:
> "Suppose, Lord Russell, this film were to be looked at by our descendants, like a Dead Sea scroll in a thousand years' time. What would you think it's worth telling that generation about the life you've lived, and the lessons you've learned from it?"
>
> Bertrand Russell:
> "I should like to say two things, one intellectual, and one moral. The intellectual thing I should want to say to them is this: When you are studying any matter or considering any philosophy, ask yourself only, 'What are the facts, and what is the truth that the facts bear out?' Never let yourself be diverted

either by what you wish to believe or by what you think would have beneficent social effects if it were believed. But look only, and solely, at what are the facts. That is the intellectual thing that I should wish to say.

"The moral thing I should wish to say to them is very simple. I should say love is wise, hatred is foolish. In this world, which is getting more and more closely interconnected, we have to learn to tolerate each other. We have to learn to put up with the fact that some people say things we don't like. We can only live together in that way. If we are to live together, and not die together, we must learn a kind of charity and a kind of tolerance which is absolutely vital to the continuation of human life on this planet."

4. What Does Winning Look Like?

"Heads I win, tails you lose."
Idiom

♪ Mr. Pinstripe Suit | Big Bad Voodoo Daddy

If liberals get what we want, what does that look like really? I don't just mean getting Democrats in the three branches of government. What do we actually want to accomplish? It's easy to get distracted by the battle, only to later realize you don't know what to do after you've won.

The truth is, even though we all identify as liberals or Democrats, we won't agree on all of the details. Does this mean we'll need to split into different factions within ourselves? Start something like the two-party system within the Democratic Party? Why just two? How about the far left versus the left versus the center left versus the environmentalists, and other special interest groups?

I hope this sounds like a bad idea. I bring this up to make the point that even in the best-case scenario, we're going to need to do some introspection as a party. We'll need to define our priorities, and work together despite our differences. So far, we've discussed the importance of approaching conservatives with good faith and understanding. We need to be able to do the same when we have disagreements within our party as well.

Conservatives are showing us what not to do as they turn on each other. The far-right MAGA crowd attacks centrist conservatives like Liz Cheney, Adam Kinzinger, and Mitt Romney as RINOs (Republican in Name Only). To the MAGA crowd, these aren't "real" conservatives. To them, "real conservatism" started with Trump. Everyone else is the swamp, including us Democrats of course. Cheney, Kinzinger, and Romney maintained their integrity and put country over party.

Though historically you wouldn't see me supporting a Cheney, we as Democrats must respect the difference between these principled conservative politicians with honor, and the majority who joined the MAGA bandwagon to protect themselves. This fissure has led to conservatives like Cheney actively opposing the Republican nominee, Donald Trump. If centrist conservatives like Cheney are able to fracture their party into two camps, MAGA and traditional Republicans, it would be great for us as Democrats. It would all but guarantee our victory in the next election.

While we could celebrate this turmoil in the Republican Party because it benefits us in the short run, this is bad for the long-term health of our country. What we are witnessing is a kind of "purge" or "purification" where those at the fringes claim to define what it means to be a "true" Republican. Trump attempted to facilitate this purge in the lead-up to the 2022 midterm elections. He made an effort to support primary challengers against centrist conservatives who weren't loyal to him.

This is an old tool in the playbook of gangsters and bullies. Vladimir Putin, Donald Trump, and Elizabeth Holmes all use it. They make examples out of those who challenge them to keep others with less of a backbone in fear. "You saw what happened to

Liz Cheney and others who wouldn't kiss the ring. Support me, or be replaced by someone who will." That's the message Trump was trying to send.

To spineless conservative politicians with a self-interest bias, that's a good argument. Cheney resisted. She was removed, and her replacement doesn't resist. They would ask what's the difference between this outcome and Cheney just capitulating in the first place? Not much, except Cheney is out of power.

Though the conservative politicians doing this mental calculus are spineless, self-interested, and weak, it's important to remember that they're also scared. You know who they wish would save them? Us. As soon as they see their electorates moving away from Trump, they'll move right alongside them, and try to act like that's where they were the whole time.

Fear is the bully's objective. They don't actually want a fight, certainly not a fair one. Bullies are scared too. They're scared, but they play the confidence game to intimidate others into submission. The end goal of a bully's fear campaign is absolute loyalty to the bully, and conformity within the group. Anyone who deviates noticeably from the norm is exiled, usually at great personal cost.

How do you face a bully? You show that you're not afraid of them, preferably in public. You fight the bully. Even if you lose, you win because the bully doesn't want to fight. The bully wins when you accept him. When you get used to the "new normal."

Cheney may have lost the battle by losing her seat in Congress, but Trump doesn't want to have to fight many more battles like that. He hopes you saw that one, and you assume he'll win the next one too. This is why he had to deny his loss in the 2020 election. If you know he can lose, the power of his intimidation diminishes. The myth becomes the man, who becomes an insecure child. The confidence game is a fragile one indeed.

Fortunately, we liberals don't have the influence of a bully instigating a "purification" within our party. Unfortunately, people in groups are prone to engage in this type of behavior anyway when left to their own devices. Purification results in division. The people who are exiled from the in-group usually still exist. They band together, and you end up with two groups of "enemies" who not long ago were on the same side. Conflict with people you obviously could have been friends with, because you just were.

I hope humans become wise enough to not always need a "common enemy" to unite us, but it's true that any squabbling we do among ourselves simply makes us more likely to hand the reins over to Republicans. This should not be the reason we show understanding and tolerance for each other, but it is a reality of our situation.

I believe we made this mistake with the left's lukewarm support of Hillary Clinton when she ran against Donald Trump in 2016. Some of us wanted to make a statement by not showing up to vote at all, or by voting for a third-party candidate. After all, if they can reliably expect our vote, why would they listen to us? It's not an unreasonable argument at face value. However, if these individuals supported the party's candidate instead of trying to make a statement, we could have swung three Supreme Court seats in our favor, and locked in a liberal court for the better part of the twenty-first century. Now we have the opposite problem. The Supreme Court has struck down abortion rights and affirmative action in college admissions. Other issues like gay marriage could be next.

This is not meant to demonize those of us who weren't fans of Hillary Clinton. My point isn't about the Clintons specifically. It's about the real-life consequences of us splitting up and losing to Republicans because of it. If our party splits up, we lose to the other party. If our nation splits up, we lose to other nations. If our alliances split up, we lose to other alliances. The fundamentals are the same, the context just gets bigger. What is the biggest context?

Legislation over Feelings

"Don't clap, vote."

Obama used to repeat this quite frequently on the campaign trail. This simple statement is one of the most impactful things I've heard him say. Given the eloquence of the forty-fourth president, that means a lot. In politics, few things disappoint me more than speaking with someone who showed up to all the protests, posted all the hashtags, chanted all the catchphrases, and proceeded not to vote in the subsequent election.

Critical race theory is a term that is so frequently misunderstood, I don't recommend using it. Even if one understands the academically correct definition of it, liberals and conservatives often end up talking past each other on this topic anyway. As such, I won't bother with the true definition. To conservatives, this term represents their fear that the government is trying to make their children racist by indoctrinating them with identity politics in schools. Not just racist generally, racist against White people specifically. This often means racist against themselves and their families. The critical race theory narrative is a tool that conservative pundits and politicians use to scare their base into voting.

Pathos (emotion) appeals may not be quite as effective as *ethos* (character) appeals at persuasion generally, but they are very good catalysts for action. In a discussion with a friend, he indicated his desire to lose all emotion so he only had logic. Though I respect the sentiment, I pushed back because without emotion, nothing would matter. Without emotion, you wouldn't care if your own mother passed away. We'd practically be inanimate objects like computers.

Wanting to do anything is an emotion. Since *pathos* is so powerful as a catalyst for action, it's not surprising that politics has become inundated with fear and hatred on both sides. I believe love is more powerful than both, but it's more difficult to generate, unfortunately.

Liberal comedian Bill Maher jokingly stated that his position on critical race theory was that "it's critical to win races." It's not critical to virtue signal. It's not critical to chant slogans in the street. Suppose one of the "I'd rather be a Russian than a Democrat" conservatives mistakenly voted for Democrats on their ballot. That conservative would have helped us more than the people who attended the protests did if they didn't vote.

Do we expect to annoy our government into some good legislation? To guilt Mitch McConnell into passing our bills? To scream at the Supreme Court until they restore Roe v. Wade? Keep dreaming. Core to Maher's argument was the concept that "power begets power." It's like an arm wrestle. Initially, when both competitors' hands are vertical and wrists are straight, it's a fair contest. However, as you begin to lose, you also have to fight against your opponent's body weight as gravity starts working against you. Imagine you start an arm wrestle with your hand only two inches off the table on your side, about to lose. This is what Maher meant by "power begets power."

Here are a few examples of Democrats being victims of Republican power in the system itself. Since the United States has had the modern two-party system, there have only been four instances where the presidential candidate who received the most votes lost the election due to the electoral college.

What Does Winning Look Like?

- Clinton vs Trump, 2016
- Gore vs Bush, 2000
- Cleveland vs Harrison, 1888
- Tilden vs Hayes, 1876

In case you, like me, could improve your knowledge of American history, every time this happened it was the Democratic candidate who won the popular vote and lost the presidency.

The United States House of Representatives has 435 voting members. In 2016, Democrats received 48% of the vote nationally compared to 49% for Republicans. If representation were proportional to votes, we would have ended up with 215 Democratic representatives, and 220 Republican representatives. In reality, we ended up with 194 Democratic representatives and 241 Republican representatives.

From 1992 to 2020, the Republican presidential candidate won the popular vote a grand total of one time—Bush versus Kerry in 2004. Contrast that with the fact that over the same time period both parties successfully nominated the same number of justices to the Supreme Court. Basically, if Democrats barely win, we still lose. Conservatives get to play with a handicap.

Republicans in my state of Ohio tried to sneak in an advantage like this during an off-year special election in 2023. It was called *Issue 1*, and the goal was to require a 60% threshold instead of a simple majority for making amendments to the state constitution. If successful, Democrats would have to win with a 60% supermajority instead of a simple majority going forward. Ironically, Issue 1 itself was a proposed amendment to the constitution. Conservatives would only need to win with a 50.01% simple majority once to force us to win by a 60% supermajority going forward indefinitely. Fortunately, it didn't pass, but they did try. This is why it's important to vote.

An understandable first instinct is to think that these conservatives are cheating. That they're not playing the political power game fairly. This is somewhat true, but what is complaining about it going to do? With the exception of the Electoral College, we can do similar things. We can gerrymander with the goal of receiving more representation than we receive votes. In 2022, we actually got 2 more representatives out of the 435 than we should have based on the percentage of votes we received nationally. It's not much, but the system was actually working in our favor for once!

In most of this book I urge us to seek friendship, common ground, and understanding with conservatives. That's for us, regular people. As it relates to legislation, our politicians need to be ruthless. Mitch McConnell is a prime example. I don't like him from a policy perspective, but I can't argue he isn't effective for the GOP.

When faced with a machine like McConnell, we can't afford to fight with gloves on and one hand tied behind our backs. There is honor in not wanting to stoop to their level. I respect it, but politicians are big boys and girls. They need to play the game, and play to win. Republican politicians are going to do so whether ours are or not.

Put down the Sledgehammer

What does winning look like? To me, it looks like making our country and, if possible, the world a better place. According to this definition, we've been doing quite well in the big picture. During the infancy of our nation, "All men are created equal" meant "men" literally. Not only that, only White men. But wait, there's more, only White men with property.

The North and the South couldn't agree on how human we were as Black people. The Southerners wanted it both ways, to treat us as property since we were slaves, but count us as people so they get more representatives. The North argued that if we were property without rights, why should we count in the state population? The South couldn't count livestock in their population, and they treated Black slaves practically the same. They settled on three-fifths. Each Black person was worth three-fifths of a White person for the purposes of counting the state population.

When you compare our country before Black people had full civil rights in the 1950s to the country as it was in the early 1800s, it's a huge leap forward. Slavery was abolished, and everyone could vote. Fast-forward to the 1970s after the civil rights movement when Jim Crow had ended. There was no more segregation, and there were antidiscrimination laws for the workplace. This is a huge leap forward from the 1950s.

Fast-forward to 2016. Most people, even conservatives, were fine with gay marriage. We had affirmative action programs to support underprivileged minorities in higher education. Mental health was taken more seriously, and the entire LGBTQ community was more accepted than it had ever been in the past. Sure, after losing three Supreme Court justices we're starting to move in the wrong direction, but overall, I'm proud of our progress.

Dr. Martin Luther King Jr. said, "The arc of the moral universe is long but it bends towards justice." This is what winning looks like. I know it feels good to complain about how terrible things are, but the truth is that we have been doing a lot of winning. If you look at where we started from, it's difficult to deny this.

Winning to me looks like that long arc of the moral universe bending toward justice, the country and the world improving slowly over time. This definition of winning is fairly boring. It doesn't quite have that *pathos* appeal to inspire and rally people to action.

This approach is like a doctor with a scalpel, making small careful changes after consulting with the experts. Then monitoring the effects of those changes to determine if any new information should alter our approach. I'm talking about a scientific approach to policy. The goal would be to inch that moral arc toward justice bit by bit with high confidence in each small move we make.

Many of my fellow liberals have a more aggressive definition of winning. They would prefer to move like a revolutionary with a sledgehammer. Breaking the arc and placing it directly where they feel it should be. It's a bit unfair of me to compare my approach to that of a doctor, and their approach to some emotional revolutionary. After all, the doctor must be the wise one, right? The scalpel and the sledgehammer are both fine tools. Though I suspect we would agree that they are tools for different situations.

If we're talking about criminal sex trafficking rings, drug cartels, or other clearly bad activities, feel free to use the sledgehammer. No need to slowly and carefully deal with them. Even with regard to the United States back when it was legal to own slaves; I'm happy taking a sledgehammer to slavery. However, the United States today is not some third world, lawless country where might makes right and the entire system needs a sledgehammer. When most of a thing is wrong, consider hitting it with a sledgehammer. When most of a thing is right, it's time for the scalpel to get the few pieces we missed.

In our current state, we're more likely to break something good that we may not even fully understand, than we are to fix something bad when hitting the system with a sledgehammer. Let's discuss a couple of examples, starting with the concept of universal basic income (UBI).

The sledgehammer approach to UBI would be to just start sending people $1,000 per month nationally and hoping our government can figure out how to pay for it later. Perhaps it will work out. Perhaps it ruins the country's economy for the foreseeable future. We can't afford to take this kind of risk.

If someone wants the federal government to implement UBI, it should be put through rigorous testing at the municipal level first. Cities that support national UBI should be willing to take the risk, and the responsibility for such experiments. Try it in a city that wants it, and see how the expense of paying everyone every month impacts net tax revenue. Does the local government earn more back in taxes than it spent on UBI? If not, was the economic stimulation worth the decline in tax revenue? Did citizens invest more in developing their skills or formal education during the experiment? What did we learn about the expected impact on inflation if this experiment were scaled? Which, if any, social programs did the city cut spending for in order to budget room for UBI? What risks do we incur relying on this experimental data that could be different if implemented on a national scale? Do we have good control cities to compare the experimental results to during the same period of time?

We need to answer all of the above questions for a given city, and then repeat the process again in other cities that will have different variables. Some variables that could change include the monthly dollar amount of UBI, whether it's in an urban or rural location, which, if any, social programs were cut to fund it, the duration of the experiment, etc. After running a few tests like these, we can see how well the UBI supporters' theories align with experimental results. More importantly, we can learn about the impact of UBI without having to bet the farm first.

It's not wise to take a leap of faith with one of the largest economies in human history. This is an example of treating policy like a scientific process. I'd even recommend getting economists to put the results of these municipal UBI experiments through peer review. This way it's not just Fox News telling us it's bad, and MSNBC telling us it's good. Economists don't always agree as often as you would hope, but still, it's the best we have. I'm not a fan of UBI in the current economy, and I'm in no hurry to run municipal experiments either. However, if someone does want UBI implemented federally, we shouldn't do so until we have strong experimental municipal data supporting it.

As it relates to the careful, scientific approach above, I want to emphasize that this level of care isn't needed for *every* change. It's only needed for high-impact changes that we haven't made before. For example, if we want to start a program to fix roads, bridges, and energy infrastructure, we can do it without experiments because we've done it many times before. When we want to do something large and new, it comes with risk. In my opinion, it would usually be irresponsible to assume this risk without testing things on a smaller scale first.

Another good example to discuss is climate change. I'm strongly for protecting the environment. I believe climate change is real, and it is human-caused. I believe we can make changes to limit how bad it will be in the future. With all of that said, if someone argued, "Let's get to net zero emissions by 2027," I'd question that person's judgment.

It's easy to say, "Let's protect the environment. They want to hit the target by 2040? I want to hit it by 2027; that means I'm more virtuous." Achieving net zero emissions within a few years would require so many drastic changes so quickly it would either be impossible or cause great destruction in society, or both.

Why net zero specifically? Because zero sounds good? How about 75% less than now? That's pretty good too, right? Often there are diminishing returns when it comes to fixing a problem. If you want to get the dirt off your car, you could wash it and get 80% off in fifteen minutes. Maybe 95% off within an hour. But going from 95% to 98% may take another hour as you carefully scrape dirt from minor cracks and crevasses. Going from 98% to 99.9% may take days, if you can even do it at all, since dirt will continue building up as you're cleaning.

Given the truth that most problems have diminishing returns as you approach perfection, why does it have to be net zero? Surely, we could do much better without being net zero. My argument isn't that net zero is a bad target necessarily. There are ways to remove carbon dioxide from the environment that make net zero possible. "Net zero" doesn't mean zero carbon emissions ever.

The point isn't about the details specifically. The point is that there are details specifically. If you aren't thinking at that level of granularity, you shouldn't be making policy. Practically no one makes policy except politicians. For normal people, it means you should have some intellectual humility and not be so confident in your opinions if you haven't thought about them at this level of detail. This is because when you are at this level of detail, many new questions arise. Reasonable questions like, if we can get 75% of the reductions with x amount of effort, but going from 75% to 90% is going to take $8x$ effort, and going from 90% to 98% is going to take $30x$ effort, which do we choose?

Thinking about problems at the detailed implementation level allows us to solve them in a responsible way. Too often, people think they can solve complex problems relying only on names, platitudes, and broad principles. Building a wall isn't a comprehensive strategy for reining in illegal immigration. The term "no child left behind" on its own doesn't mean that education will be better because of it. The Affordable Care Act doesn't necessarily guarantee that care will be affordable. My point isn't that everything above is bad; it's that if you only know some names and a few principles, it's not enough to justify confidence.

When it comes to policy, the devil is in the details. In most cases, people are too busy to dig into them. This is a fact of life, and it doesn't mean we shouldn't have opinions anyway. It means we shouldn't get married to those opinions.

The True Power of Science

I strongly support a scientific approach to policy, and asking the scientific community for their input on policy decisions. Though many of us trust our science institutions, there is a growing crowd that has its reservations. The politicized nature of COVID-19 recently dealt serious damage to the reputation of science, especially in conservative circles. We have two camps, one faithful to science, and the other skeptical of science. There is a possibility that both sides could learn more about the true power of science.

A common mistake I see people make is putting too much value in the wisdom, character, or intelligence of an individual person. Donald Trump is a good example with his argument of "only I can fix it." When someone tells you only they can fix something, it implies that either they have a monopoly on good ideas, which itself is a bad idea, or that they're the only non-corrupt person, which is almost always incorrect as well.

People have a tendency to conflate success in one part of life, usually one involving generating wealth, with being generally intelligent. There is certainly a correlation between the two. However, my experience is that most people are about average in intelligence regardless of their wealth level. Some people do well because they are generally intelligent. Others do well because they are good at one or two specific things.

Paul is a successful musician who has earned millions of dollars in his career. By earnings, some people would expect him to be generally intelligent. He may be, but he could just be good at making music that his audience wants to hear. If this is the case, we shouldn't put more stock in his opinion on something like climate change than we would the opinion of a random person off the street. It's not like Paul is a climate scientist, right?

Actually, the individual climate scientist may be no more generally intelligent than Paul, a businessman, or a random person off the street either. An individual scientist's opinion on something like climate change isn't sacrosanct. The power of science doesn't lie in the expert knowledge or supposed superior intellect of the scientist.

Scientists are normal people like us who chose to become scientists. The true power of science lies in the scientific community via peer review. Scientists are not immune to the influence of bias. Scientists are fully capable of having bad ideas. However, it's very difficult to get your biases and bad ideas past peer review, and then become the default agreed-upon perspective of the community of scientists in your field.

The fundamentals of this are why the only conspiracy theories that are plausible to me are small ones. The bigger a conspiracy is, the less likely it is to be true. If there is a conspiracy that requires a group of three friends to be secretly plotting something nefarious, that's plausible. If the conspiracy is that the nation of China doesn't exist, it's just too large, and too many people would have to be in on it for it to be feasible. If China weren't real, then the conspiracy would have to be so big that my own wife would be engaged in it. Sure, I've never been to China personally, but there's no practical way that many people are participants in a conspiracy.

Don't confuse this with an argument that "if a lot of people believe something, it must be true." A lot of people can be wrong about something together, but a conspiracy entails deceit, secrecy, and lies. These things are unstable at scale. It would be like trying to share a secret in a game of telephone with x number of people. Then expecting that your secret has been communicated properly with everyone, and that no one told anybody else. I can't think of ten people I know that I could trust to execute that properly.

A conspiracy with over a thousand people in on it? I'm highly skeptical. Someone could argue that the truth does get out, that's why we're aware of the conspiracy. This is possible, but it usually only takes one or two people who were in on a conspiracy to talk in order to bring it down. This is why criminals hate and punish people who "snitch." One snitch can bring down your entire organization. One intern's stained dress almost brought down the president of the United States, Bill Clinton. Unless you also believe the conspiracy that everyone in power is in on all the conspiracies, you should be highly skeptical of any large, long-lasting conspiracy.

Likewise, a single educated scientist with some bad ideas, biases, or who was being paid off by corporate interests could spread misinformation. Even a handful of scientists could do this. But I don't think any group in the world has enough money to get some idiocy scientists know is wrong past peer review, and then end up with anything near a majority opinion on it.

How much money would it take to get not a consensus, just 51% of geologists or climate scientists to publish in their papers that the earth is flat? Even if you by some miracle pulled it off once, science builds on top of itself. If the earth is flat, that revelation impacts other science. Future theories would need to be built somehow on top of the false premise that the earth is flat. Now you have to pay off the vast majority of scientists everywhere forever to continue marketing a lie, when anyone can see the truth with their own eyes. This is practically impossible.

What is possible, however, is to mislead the general population, which doesn't understand how science works. Perhaps the most frequently misunderstood aspect of science is the term *consensus*. When some people hear the word consensus, they think, "Consensus is a lie, not all scientists agree." This is a persuasive argument because it's true. Using the example of climate change, not all scientists agree that climate change is caused by human activities. Some may not even agree that climate change is happening at all. However, this is only the end of the discussion if you view "consensus" as a binary true or false claim. If it's binary, then there can be no consensus on anything in the world, unless you're talking about a small group of people.

If you describe consensus in more detail with numbers, you can end up with information like x% of scientists believe y thing is happening for z reason. When the value of x becomes north of 95%, I think it's fair to call that a consensus. Sure, the 5% could be right, but it would be irresponsible for us to see a 95% to 5% split, and then act like it's a toss-up. Unfortunately, even in the face of numbers like 99% to 1%, it's very easy for the media to manipulate us. All they need to do is show us one scientist from the 1% side and one scientist from the 99% side. Then the media looks "fair and balanced" because they showed "both sides."

Normal people could watch the program and understandably leave afterward feeling like scientists are still divided on the topic. They will respect this news channel for giving them both sides, and trusting them to make an informed decision. Ironically, they will think the news channels that didn't do this are pushing propaganda. They may think that anyone who's too confident is being foolish or worse, intentionally pushing a narrative for their own benefit. This is a gateway to further pessimism and conspiracy thinking. The layperson believes they're seeing evidence of it due to the fact that the other news stations only show the 99% side.

Suppose ninety-eight out of one hundred auto mechanics agree that you need to replace your car's engine. The two mechanics who disagree work for the insurance company responsible for paying for the replacement. The insurance company asks the news station to show one mechanic from "both sides" in order to manufacture uncertainty.

Even better, the news station invites both mechanics from the insurance company, and one from the other ninety-eight. Watching the program, it looks like two out of three mechanics are on the insurance company's side. It's funny, but it's also a shame. It's nearly impossible to corrupt ninety-eight out of one hundred auto mechanics in a conspiracy. It's much easier, and more affordable, to corrupt two who work for you, and then confuse people into inaction. It's our job as a society to not be foolish enough to fall for it.

In addition to not understanding why the scientific consensus is nearly incorruptible, some science skeptics argue that science is often wrong. This is both true and false, depending on the context.

If you're reading science textbooks, I expect that over 95% of that information is correct, and will not need to be changed for the rest of time going forward. In this context, science is not often wrong. Public science enthusiast and educator Dr. Neil DeGrasse Tyson compared our scientific knowledge to a circle. The area inside the circle represents things we have already learned. The perimeter of the circle is where what we know meets the unknown.

New scientific discoveries happen at the perimeter. The content near the center of the circle usually has a long history. Those things have been well tested directly and indirectly in multiple different experiments over time. The content near the perimeter is usually less certain. It often has a shorter history, and fewer experiments backing it up. As scientists stand on the perimeter and hypothesize about what lies in the unknown abyss in front of them, the majority of their ideas will be wrong.

I believe this is why Albert Einstein said, "Imagination is more important than knowledge." Knowledge can get you to the edge of the circle. However, being at the edge doesn't help the scientific community advance. You help the scientific community advance by expanding the circle. We don't know what lies in the space outside the circle. We have to use imagination, creativity, and original thought to create what the truth could be in our minds. Then we devise experiments that validate or invalidate our hypothesis. Running this experiment and finding out your hypothesis was wrong is still valuable. It makes you another step closer to finding out what's right.

The unfortunately politicized COVID-19 saga ended up being bad marketing for science. This is because studying a new virus that changes and forms new variants in real time causes scientists to operate at the perimeter of the circle, which most of us never see. The public usually only sees science when it manifests in their lives as part of some product a businessperson made with scientific technology after it was already proven.

After seeing how messy, uncertain, and error-prone scientific work is at the perimeter, it made people lose faith in science generally. Scientists will be wrong a lot at the perimeter, but they're rarely wrong near the center of the circle. When determining the best public policy for a new disease, scientists will likely make some mistakes. When determining what happens when hydrogen and oxygen interact with each other, they are probably not going to get it wrong.

Does this mean we shouldn't listen to scientists when they are working at the perimeter? No. They are the experts, and if work is getting past peer review, I can't think of a more credible source than their majority or consensus opinion. Anyone claiming to have a better perspective than a peer-reviewed process by the experts has too much confidence in themselves, even if hindsight ends up proving them correct.

Reasonable People Can Disagree

To reduce tribalism, it's important to understand when to draw a line in the sand, and when to relax, accepting that reasonable people can disagree. In politics, the variety of opinions you will encounter is practically infinite, even within a political party. If every time you have a difference of opinion, you decide to draw a line in the sand and create a war out of it, it's difficult to turn down the temperature. It also makes people in the center uncomfortable joining us because they don't fit into the left's current definition of perfection. This makes our tent smaller, and makes us more likely to lose elections.

Suppose Kelly and Martin are forced to cook fries together. Kelly shakes some salt onto the fries and then stops. Martin wants to add two more shakes of salt. They then get into a heated feud, passionately arguing back and forth about the right amount of salt to be added to the fries.

Eventually, this dispute results in Kelly accusing Martin of having poor taste and intellect. This makes Martin feel justified in responding back with further ad hominem insults. The next thing you know, they're physically attacking each other over the disrespect generated from the salt dispute.

This sounds ridiculous, but large conflicts arise from small conflicts all the time. This is made more likely when the parties didn't like or respect each other in the first place. This would be the case if Kelly were a liberal and Martin were a conservative.

This was a battle that simply was not worth fighting. Two shakes of salt is within the range of reasonable disagreement. Neither person was suggesting they dump the whole carton of salt on the fries. No one was savage enough to suggest unsalted fries. For those extreme scenarios, I'd understand drawing a line in the sand, or in the fries. However, for plus or minus two shakes, just accept that you disagree, and that neither side is being unreasonable.

If we turn down the temperature, we might even be able to compromise and just do one more shake of salt. Then we could live together in peace, enjoying some mostly good, yet imperfect fries. Instead, we are rolling around fighting each other while the fries are being burned so badly no one will want to eat them.

In a modern society where you have to interact with other people, your fries are almost never going to have the perfect amount of salt. You don't have to be OK with your fries being spoiled or dirty. You will, however, have to endure less than optimal salt levels. You might have to eat crinkle-cut fries when you prefer straight-cut or curly fries. Even if you choose to fight, you're still not going to get everything you want. I recommend picking your battles carefully.

Let's get out of hypothetical analogy land and into some real issues. In the past we've disagreed on the following questions. Democrats weren't always on the right side of these disputes.

- Should the United States allow slavery?
- Should women be able to vote?
- Should Black people have civil rights?
- Should gay people be able to get married?

These are line-in-the-sand battles I can understand fighting for. In all of these battles, we won. Not Democrats, the country. Now take a look at some modern disagreements we have with conservatives.

- Is it OK for White people to appropriate Black culture?
- Can Black people be racist?
- How much affirmative action in college admissions is too much?
- Should we have to call people by their preferred pronouns?
- Which bathrooms should trans people use?

Of course, there are other disagreements in the modern era on things like tax rates, social programs, and foreign policy. However, these are popular culture war issues that stir up a lot of hatred today. Despite the emotion behind them, they are pretty small when compared to the issues of the past.

Who does cultural appropriation hurt, and how much does

it hurt them? How much lower should a Black person be able to score on an entrance exam and still get in, over an equivalent White person? Five percent lower? Fifteen percent lower? They should be treated identically? To me, none of these opinions are unreasonable. Unreasonable would be something like 30% lower, or test scores not mattering at all. Someone who supports affirmative action will disagree with someone who is against it, but neither of them is ridiculous. They just have slightly different values.

Total agreement among everyone is impossible. The best we can do is arrive at a point where the only disagreements that exist are between reasonable alternatives. If we push too far and demand submission on issues where reasonable people can disagree, not only do we risk becoming wrong ourselves, we risk losing elections due to extreme policies that alienate the electorate.

Let's spectate Vicky, a loving mother to her daughter Lacey. Vicky's son-in-law, Jake, physically abuses Lacey. He is also an alcoholic. Vicky has some serious and important work to do. Assuming Jake and Lacey stay married, the first priority for Vicky is to get him to stop the abuse (slavery). Let's say she succeeds, and Jake stops the violence. Great, but he's still an alcoholic (women can't vote and there is no gay marriage). She convinces him to stop drinking too. Fantastic!

Now her major concerns are solved, but she still doesn't like Jake due to his history of abusing her daughter. Understandable. Because of this, she continues to nitpick at everything he does. Why don't you shave more often (cultural appropriation)? You should go to bed earlier (call people by their preferred pronouns). You're too lazy and don't make enough money (he doesn't support affirmative action).

Vicky had a real reason to hate Jake before. Now, even if she is right about some things, she's not the type of person you want to associate with. When Jake's friends come over to have a beer and joke around, they see Vicky looking down her nose at them in disgust. Do you think any of them would vote for her if she were running for office? Of course not.

Are they all unworthy, bad people she shouldn't want support from anyway? If you think so, that's more small-tent pessimism that will cause us to lose moving forward. If she shows a little good faith and appreciation for the improvements Jake made, he's more likely to listen to the rest of her advice.

We can practice where to draw the line with the topic of race. We'll start off with Black people being literally enslaved. Obviously, the right direction is to support Black people. Next, we're not slaves, but there are Jim Crow laws and we don't have civil rights. Still, the right direction is clearly to support Black people. After 1964, Black people have civil rights, but there is still evidence of systemic issues. Things like Black families getting worse terms and higher rejection rates for bank loans compared to similar White families. The right move is still to support Black people, but it's less clear than slavery or civil rights was.

Next, we notice that Black people aren't being accepted into universities at rates we would expect. Some propose affirmative action programs to have more diverse campuses. Is it correct to support Black people in this regard? Personally, I'm fine with it, but a reasonable person could have the opposite view and I'd respect it.

How should we feel about diversity quotas in companies to ensure no discrimination is going on? Forcing companies to hire certain types of people at certain rates is delicate business. On one hand, the civil rights act of 1964 has protections against discrimination in the workplace; how do you enforce it without tracking things like the number of certain types of people at specific levels inside companies? On the other hand, a company feeling forced to hire token Black people to look good is a bad thing, assuming they weren't discriminating in the first place.

I'm OK with some sort of quota if it's a very low bar, like you can't have ten thousand employees and no people of color. Or, if you're a large corporation and we learn there is an unspoken policy that no people of color can be above a certain rank, and the numbers indicate evidence of this truth. Besides these very low bars, it feels more wrong to have significant quotas than it does to have none.

Continuing further, what should our stance be on social programs that would benefit Black people specifically? What if we provided extra childcare funding and early education opportunities for Black children with the goal of closing the wealth gap Black families have with White families? I appreciate the sentiment here as a biased Black person, but singling out Black kids for educational benefits that no one else gets feels wrong to me. It is trying to right wrong in the past with an opposite wrong in the present.

Let's end with the topic of reparations. Should all Black people who are descendants of slaves be compensated for injustices to their ancestors? How much is a life of enslavement worth? Ignoring the logistical challenges of determining who is actually a descendant of slaves, and calculating the dollar amount each eligible Black person would be owed, it's still a bad policy where reasonable people can't disagree, in my opinion.

The best argument I've heard in support of reparations goes like this. If someone harms someone else, they can be sued. If the court rules in favor of the plaintiff, the defendant will owe them compensatory and sometimes punitive monetary damages. If the plaintiff ends up dying, the defendant's responsibility to pay damages doesn't go away. He would owe the family of the plaintiff, their spouse or children. This is how our current legal system works.

It's not a stretch to accept that enslaving someone harms them. Almost everyone supports the concept of payment for damages. Likewise, nearly all of us agree that money owed should go to one's family if they are deceased. Based on this simple foundation that most people would agree with, the conclusion is that Black people are owed reparations.

That line of reasoning appears sound to me. However, it's incomplete. Even if we agree that Black people deserve reparations based on the argument above, no one alive today deserves to pay reparations. The best counterargument I've heard is that it's the government that owes Black people, not the people of today. I understand that abstractly. However, practically speaking, it's the non-Black people of today whose tax revenue would be paying for it despite receiving no benefits from it, and not being responsible for it. It would be punishing the people of today for the sins of their fathers. In many cases, even for White citizens, their "fathers" may have had nothing to do with slavery. Some of their ancestors were participants in the underground railroad who put their own families' well-being at risk for Black people. Many of them fought the Confederates in the Civil War in order to end slavery. Should their descendants owe reparations?

Once you have a position like "support Black people," it's easy to stay with it too long and end up in some tricky or outright immoral positions, despite starting on very solid ground. We don't want to become the annoying mother-in-law who complains no matter how much you improve. We still have some work to do, and we need to protect the gains we've made. With that said, most of our problems today are simply much smaller than the problems we've had in the past. Our confidence and passion to fight on every issue should diminish accordingly.

Fundamentally, it doesn't matter if Democrats are in office. It only matters that we make our country better over time. Abraham Lincoln was a Republican at a time when Democrats were a racist, pro-slavery party. We don't make the country better by posting hashtags and marching through the streets. These activities raise awareness for sure, but raising awareness only gets the ball in our court. We haven't scored until we pass legislation. The only way to reliably pass the legislation we want is to get more of us in the government by voting.

Suppose we implement some of the changes in this book and begin winning more elections. After losing repeatedly, Republicans realize they have to abandon the far right, and move toward the center. After repositioning toward the center, Republicans finally win an election.

If this happened, it wouldn't be that bad because Republicans would have become more worthy of winning. The beautiful thing is this process started because we made ourselves more worthy of winning. This means that if we don't improve as a party, we're actually helping the far right by not punishing them for their extremism and allowing them to win.

It should be clear to the vast majority of Americans that we're the better choice. If we can't successfully make this case to the American people, the far right will become even more powerful. In this regard, we have the power to defeat right-wing extremism. With great power comes great responsibility.

5. Personal Contexts

"When you're smiling, the whole world smiles with you."
— Louis Armstrong

♪ Colors | Black Pumas

Growing up, the boys on my mom's side of the family would sometimes spend weekends at my uncle's apartment. Many families are blessed to have a cool uncle, I was fortunate enough to have a few. These weekends were an opportunity for the guys to hang out, joke around, play video games, and eat unhealthy food. Good times.

One particular weekend, we were up late the night before and I was sleeping in the living room. Around five in the morning I heard the phone ring. This was a house phone, for those old enough to remember them. Since I was a guest, I wasn't going to answer it. I decided to lie there and let it ring. My uncle was dead asleep, so I figured he wasn't going to answer it either. However, after a few seconds I heard him leap out of bed and scramble to reach the phone before it stopped ringing.

It was early in the morning and no lights were on, so it was hard to see. In his haste to reach the phone, he stubbed his toe very hard on a piece of furniture and almost fell down. This is when I started laughing. He cursed. He recovered in time to pick up the phone and angrily yell, "Hello?" The poor telemarketer on the other end had no idea what he just walked into. Let's just say he received quite an earful, and probably wouldn't be calling back again. It wasn't a pleasant moment for my uncle or the telemarketer, but I had a good laugh at the brief, unexpected comedy show.

No one wants to talk to telemarketers, but if he had called a few hours later, he would have interacted with a much more pleasant version of my uncle. Such is the power of context. By context, I mean everything in the background that influences your perception of the world. This is a necessarily broad definition because it is impossible to list everything that makes up the frame of our experience.

There are deep, society-level contexts that people of a nation or culture share, and there are contexts unique to the individual's identity. In this chapter, we're going to explore the power of context at the individual level. Understanding contexts is key to understanding each other. Understanding each other is half of the recipe for combatting tribalism. As a reminder, the other half is good faith.

It's October 1, 2023, as I'm currently writing this, in the State of Ohio. Last night around one in the morning I stepped outside with my German shepherd, Grace, and waited for her to relieve herself. While I was waiting during this peaceful autumn evening, I looked up and took in the heavens. The moon was brighter than expected, as if it were one in the afternoon on the surface of the moon. In contrast to how dark it was outside, the moon almost hurt my eyes. So I focused instead on the countless tiny lights dotting the night sky. One of them seemed noticeably larger and brighter than the others. I wondered if it might be one of the planets visible to the naked eye.

A peaceful autumn evening with a bright full moon and an excuse to linger. This was my context. The brightness of the moon caused me to focus on the stars and sparked a sense of wonder within me. I was curious about how far away individual stars were. How many intelligent beings, if any at all, were looking at our star at this moment? Given that general relativity tells us that time is relative, what is "this moment" really? Deep, curious, even somewhat spiritual thoughts.

Thoughts that likely wouldn't have crossed my mind at all had the context been only slightly different. Imagine we keep everything the same but it's cloudy outside. This line of inquiry would not have happened. Imagine it was winter instead of autumn, and the temperature was below freezing. If it were that cold, I'd probably just be anxious to get back inside and wouldn't have taken my time perusing the night sky. Certain modes of thinking are more likely to arise in some contexts than in others.

Art has the magical power of introducing us to other contexts. I use the term "art" loosely here. Art could be literature like books, movies, poetry, or a spoken story. Art could be music, paintings, video games, the beauty of nature, etc. Works of art are portals to other contexts. I'm a big fan of music in particular. In a social setting, music can allow all of us to experience the same context, or at least a very similar one, for just a few minutes.

In life, people can be near each other looking at the same thing, but from significantly different contexts. Suppose there are three students in class, Sarah, Zoey, and Alisha. The context of Sarah's life may be most akin to a movie like *The Pursuit of Happiness*. Her family struggles with poverty, which creates conflict at home. Sarah's main goal in life is trying to appear normal to her friends, while working on a long-term strategy to avoid financial hardship.

Zoey's context is quite different; hers is more comparable to a sports movie about an athlete's journey to master her craft. Alisha is smitten with a particular boy in class. Her life resembles more of a romance drama.

Though all three girls are in the same classroom, the contexts they view life from are quite distinct. However, at a music concert listening to a band they all like, the current song could be inviting them into a spirit of revelry with high-tempo dance music. The next could be a love song that invites all of them into Alisha's romance-based context.

There is something beautiful about people sharing a positive context together; I'm grateful that art helps us do that. Though Sarah, Zoey, and Alisha have different default contexts they experience life from, the differences would likely be greater when compared to girls of their age in a country on the other side of the world. This is due to differences in the society-level context. We'll discuss the political impact of societal contexts in the next chapter.

Most contexts come with some level of what I call "inertia." Contexts with high inertia make it difficult for you to leave them to explore other contexts. Inertia can be dangerous, even debilitating when it stops us from leaving negative contexts like misery and anger.

You can do a simple experiment at home to experience inertia. Think about two songs you like. If you like them similarly as much, you may be indifferent as to which one you listen to first. Pick one. Before you get halfway through the song, you will probably feel like you made the right decision, and want to continue listening to it. At this point, you'd likely oppose the idea of switching to the other song, even though you like it about as much.

This resistance to changing the musical context you're in is inertia. Once the first song finishes, play the other one. You may find that in the first few moments of the second song, you still miss the first, because inertia is trying to keep you in that context. As you continue listening, inertia will begin to shift until it is completely within the context of the second song.

People respond to inertial forces in certain contexts differently. For instance, I'm highly sensitive to inertia in a work context. To me, the worst part of work by far is the beginning, getting started. Once I get going, work really isn't too bad. Knowing this, I try to start work as few times as possible. The consequences are that I don't enjoy suffering interruptions, and I'm bad at multitasking. It requires a high level of mental endurance to work for long hours with minimal breaks. However, once I'm done, I'm not going to endure a context switch again unless it's an emergency. In contrast, my paternal grandmother used to study off and on fifteen minutes at a time, alternating between work and play. That would annoy me to no end.

Social Contexts

Humans are social animals. Contexts exist not only around ourselves as individuals, but around ourselves in relation to others. Let's examine the social contexts of race and sex in a professional environment. Suppose three people are waiting in the lobby for a job interview that only one of them will receive. Brad is a White male, Deontay is a Black male, and Priya is an Indian female. They all experience nervousness due to their competition with each other, but for different reasons.

Priya is concerned about her ability to seem confident and strong compared to American men. English is her second language, so she has to think longer than Americans do before she responds.

She fears that this will make her look less capable than she is. Deontay is glad his first name didn't scare the company into not giving him an interview. Despite his gratitude for getting an interview at all, he has a chip on his shoulder. Deontay expects the interviewers to have low expectations for him because of his race, and feels the need to prove himself. Brad is a conservative. He's worried about being at a disadvantage because he's a White male. He knows the Black guy has diversity on his side, as does the Indian woman. He asks himself how much better he will have to do than those two to get the job.

A job interview is a stressful experience. This shared stressful context made each of them aware of their social identities along the lines of sex and race, in relation to each other. Let's entertain a different context where the three were not fighting for the same job. Instead, they had already accepted offers to work here, and they were in the lobby awaiting orientation. This is a much more comfortable context to be in. A context that is much more compatible with good faith.

The three may spark up a conversation and begin building positive relationships. Their gender or sex may not even cross their minds as relevant. It's still part of the context they view the world from, but it isn't consciously noticeable right now. Elements of our social identities always exist within us. Sometimes we don't notice them at all. Sometimes they express themselves positively or negatively. The negative side is much more likely to rear its head in more dangerous, stressful, or tribal environments.

Family is likely the most powerful and influential social context. Knowing Brad as a stranger is one thing. Knowing Brad as a brother, father, or son are other things entirely. The brother, father, and son contexts of knowing Brad are distinct from each other, but they all carry extra meaning to us compared to Brad being a random person off the street. The concept underneath the saying "Blood is thicker than water" is what I'm talking about.

When we are viewing the world in a context where Brad is a stranger, there is a certain callous indifference we will feel toward him. He is just another of the eight billion people on earth that we don't have the energy to care about. Hating Brad for his faults, or harming him if he stands in the way of our interests, are options that are on the table.

If instead Brad is your son, the odds are that he will mean the world to you. Even if Brad grows up to be a flawed man you wouldn't normally respect, you'll likely still love him, and blame yourself for not raising him better. You will see the light within Brad even though it rarely shows itself. You will have known some of the challenges he faced that led him down the wrong path. Despite all of his problems, hating him or harming him in the long run are not ideas you will entertain.

As you can see, the family context is highly compatible with good faith. Unfortunately, it doesn't usually include many people. Perhaps this is why many religions refer to humans as "God's children." That would make us brothers and sisters, which broadens the family context to include everyone. Regardless of your religious beliefs or lack thereof, trying to treat people as if they were in your family context is a noble endeavor. One that will help establish the good faith needed to combat tribalism.

The Context Switching Superpower

Earlier I mentioned that the beauty of nature could be appreciated like art. Imagine two strangers, Oasha and Ken, are next to each other on a beach in South America. They are staring at the same horizon, a sunset filled with oranges, reds, and purples. They are taking in the same smells and sounds of wildlife in the area. They are in the same physical context, and when asked how they feel, they both respond, "Peaceful." Though they both report feeling "peaceful," what they feel within could be different versions of peace entirely.

It's impossible to really connect and know how someone feels. The best Oasha can do is use words and nonverbal indicators to describe her feelings. Then Ken can search through his experiences to find an emotional state that approximates Oasha's. We can approximate, but we can never really know how someone else experiences beauty. How our mother loves us. How the musician feels when he's playing a song. Sometimes I'll be in a particularly enlightened or spiritual state, and I'll wish that I could share it with someone. I'll wonder, if I have a child, will he or she ever have the same experience? Unfortunately, I think the answer is no, but I'd be happy to be wrong.

In this section, I'd like to invite you to participate in a thought experiment. In this thought experiment, you will be granted the context switching superpower for one day. On this day, you will experience the world through the contexts of every person on earth. This means you will experience the exact same appreciation for the beauty of the sunset that they do. The same enjoyment they feel while listening to music genres you don't even like personally. You will experience every social identity. The comradery they feel with their best friends. You will experience everyone's insecurities. Everyone's pride. Everyone's love they have for their spouse. The love they have for their sons. You will also experience their bigotry and hatred. Their anger. Their passions for vengeance. Their fears. You will experience it all.

Personal Contexts

You do this. You spend a day living in each person's context. I'd be astonished if you didn't come back much wiser, much more understanding, and most importantly, full of love.

We can't actually do this thought experiment, so why does this unverifiable hypothetical matter? If you're a pessimist who believes that after understanding everyone, you'll come back a misanthrope, and hate people more than you already do, then there isn't much to gain from this experiment. I can't prove you wrong because it's hypothetical. However, if you agree with me that it's more likely for you to come back more understanding and full of love, why not just act like you're understanding and full of love anyway?

Suppose you knew with certainty that a specific stranger would be the love of your life, but at this point you haven't met them yet. That person needs your help. How do you respond? Would you treat them like a stranger because you don't actually know them? Or would you take it seriously as if they were the love of your life because you know they will be, even though you don't actually feel the love yet? I'm choosing the latter.

I don't actually feel love for you, but I'm confident that there is a context in which I would. Out of respect for that context, I'm not going to treat you in a way that the me from that context would be ashamed of. For example, I assume you love your mother. Imagine you were born as someone else who didn't know your mother at all. If that alternative version of you were to interact with your mother, wouldn't you appreciate it if you still treated your mother with love and respect? Wouldn't you be upset if that version of you ended up hurting your mother's feelings?

If you believe, as I do, that the most enlightened version of yourself has understanding, love, and respect for everyone, don't wait for the enlightenment.

Negative Contexts

In the previous section I made the assumption that after experiencing all contexts, positive and negative, in the end the positive contexts would win. Let's discuss why I believe that is the case with specific examples.

In the context switching thought experiment, you would have experienced the racism of White people who think they are superior to Black people. You also would have experienced the racism of Black people who think they are superior to White people. You would have felt both, but both can't be right. Both can, however, be foolish. You would have experienced the contexts of good men, Black and White, who are more honorable and respectable than both groups of racists.

Let's consider experiencing the context of people like the young Aaron Stark. The would-be school shooter youth who was angry, hopeless, battling depression, and prepared to lash out at society. A grim circumstance, where it's tough to see the light at the end of the tunnel. However, you also would have experienced the contexts of people like Aaron Stark, the adult, who walked out of that tunnel, and started a family. You would know that most of the time it does get better.

There are specific statistical truths about the light at the end of the tunnel that you could tell someone with depression. Unfortunately, those *logos* fact-based arguments are unlikely to have the strength to pull someone out of a negative context. To help them, you need a way to generate a context change. *Pathos* and *ethos* are much better at that. Aaron Stark didn't need a set of facts to be presented to him. He needed a friend. He needed a good time to remind him that yes, life can be good.

While we're on the topic of negative contexts, let's expand the superpower in the thought experiment. The superpower will not only include the ability to experience all existing contexts for everyone on earth, but all possible contexts each person could exist within. Eight billion contexts, one for each person on earth pales in comparison to the scope of experiencing all possible contexts. Let's focus on just a couple of the possible contexts for a good kid in our neighborhood named Billy.

In the context of our reality, Billy is well-mannered, and treats everyone with respect. We like Billy. If we were in the context of Billy's mom, we'd love Billy. Let's keep Billy otherwise the same, but change his physical build. In this new hypothetical context, he is tall and very muscular for his age, instead of average like he originally was.

In the context of Billy being large and muscular, he picked up a tendency to bully others. Billy may have a disposition toward elevating his social status with aggression that we simply were unaware of when he was normal-sized. Now that Billy is bigger, he has the confidence to express darkness within him that remained dormant in other contexts.

Billy, the bully, terrorizes his peers at school, contributing to some of them becoming suicidal. We don't like Billy the bully. We may hate him. Let's alter this hypothetical context again, and make his parents more interested in teaching him not to exercise his bullying tendencies. If they did that successfully, then Billy the bully would just be big Billy and we'd like him again.

In this example, we changed Billy's size. Instead, we could put Billy in a different hypothetical situation where his actions would cause us to judge him negatively. You don't have to try very hard to imagine a context where you could hate almost everyone. Your family, your spouse, even yourself.

I've seen siblings at each other's throats, and not always figuratively. Marriages that start off loving often end in bitter divorce. Marriage can be difficult just managing the finite amount of contexts life will throw at your relationship over six decades. In all possible contexts, I can almost guarantee there is some hypothetical situation, some sequence of events that would cause you to lose respect for or even hate your spouse.

There are contexts in which we could hate everyone. There are contexts in which we could love everyone. Does that mean nothing matters? It's all a wash? Well, I believe there are more contexts where you would love everyone than contexts where you would hate them. I can't prove that, however, and my opinion could be a result of a bias toward optimism. Assume that I'm wrong, and there are more contexts where we could hate each other than love each other. Wouldn't it be honorable to try to create the contexts where we could love each other? To try to move the world toward a context where we don't have to hate Billy?

Throughout this book, you will see me say things like, "my racist White friends." You may wonder why I call them friends. Because I'd rather move the world toward a context where I could befriend them, than remain in one where I feel justified hating them. I don't want to have to have disdain for them. The best way to move toward a context where we could be friends is to start treating them like one. Respect the box, then the box may become worthy of respect, like Aaron Stark.

6. Societal Contexts

"If you were me, you'd be doing exactly what I'm doing."
– Rasaan Hollis, age 8

♪ Sympathy for the Devil | The Rolling Stones

- Burn women at the stake ✓
- Persecute Jewish people ✓
- Purchase slaves ✓
- Believe the popular religion ✓

We're the same people. Humans—*Homo sapiens*—have been on earth for about three hundred thousand years. For many of us, our interest in history goes back no further than the year we were born. Most modern societies use the BC/AD distinction to orient our history around the life of Jesus Christ, approximately two thousand years ago.

Humans have been around a very long time compared to the length of our attention spans. However, compared to the age of the earth, 4.5 billion years, or the age of a species like crocodiles at over fifty million years, we haven't been here long at all. Genetically speaking, a human from ten thousand years ago is still a human almost exactly like you and me. You could drop one in society today as a baby, and they would blend right in.

People committed horrible atrocities in the past. Genocides, slavery, mass rape, child sacrifices, genital mutilation, the list goes on. We deplore the monsters who committed those atrocities. The unpleasant truth is that the vast majority of those "monsters" were normal people like us. Horrendous *Homo sapiens*. We are social animals. Most people will be normal people, whatever "normal" means for the society they grow up in.

Put them in an enlightened modern liberal society; they'll be enlightened, modern, and liberal. Put them in a traditionally conservative religious society; they'll be traditional, conservative, and will practice the predominant religion of that society. Put them in a society with large amounts of brutality, violence, and criminal activity, and they'll fit right in too.

This means there is potential for great darkness within us. The woke liberal of today could have been a concentration camp guard in Nazi Germany, and vice versa if their conditions were swapped. There is little biological basis to suggest that humans have changed morally based on genetics in the last ten thousand years, let alone the last few hundred.

You can look through history and find horrible societies you'd hate to be in that represent the worst of us. You can also find examples of societies that are much closer to something we'd call ideal. If the people are basically the same genetically, what explains the difference? Humans obviously have the capacity for great cruelty, but we also have the capacity for great honor. I believe the difference is due to contexts at the societal level.

Would You Have Owned Slaves?

Would you have owned slaves? If you did, would you have mated with the people you own despite them only being able to give "consent" under duress? I don't know. Despite any confidence you may have from within your current context, I don't think you know either.

I have a pet ball python named Zeus. Zeus eats mice or small rats. When I buy rats to feed them to Zeus, I feel sorry for them. I'd feel sorrier for buying Zeus and then letting him starve, but I feel sorry for the rats nonetheless. Looking into the eyes of the innocent rodent I'll soon indirectly kill, I feel the need to morally justify what I'm about to do. Let's walk through my internal justifications.

Those rats in the store were bred specifically to be fed to reptiles. If I don't buy one now, someone else will tomorrow. Their fate is sealed; the only difference is whether they'll be eaten now, or some hours or days later. Plus, I have a policy that if for some reason Zeus isn't interested in eating the mouse, or it survives due to its own agility or intellect, I'll set it free. In other words, I think I'd give the rat a better chance of survival than it would have with someone else. I doubt most other people buying rats for their reptiles are as deep within this moral dilemma as I am. What else am I going to do, let my snake starve? Am I going to buy all the rats and set them free? I don't have the money to do that at a scale that would make a significant difference.

I review my thoughts one final time before sentencing. I can't feasibly spend my life buying a bunch of rats and setting them free. Even if I don't buy this one, it will be dead soon anyway. I have a snake to take care of. This is enough to convince me to sentence the rat to death by asphyxiation.

One particular evening after I had gone through a moral justification like this again, I thought about slavery. To my horror, I realized that most of the arguments I used to justify feeding rats to my snake could be used to justify a White person purchasing slaves.

Let's start with the fact that White people purchased slaves from the store, just like I did with the rats. I'm sure the building looked different in West Africa where White slave traders purchased African slaves from other Africans, but it was a marketplace nonetheless. The majority of slaves were sold this way. For the most part, White people weren't raiding Africa to capture free people and force them into slavery. West African warlords did that upon realizing the demand for slaves in the New World in the eighteenth and nineteenth centuries.

That's a troubling prospect, isn't it? Foreign demand for slaves is so high, and there is so much money to be made, your own people create businesses capturing young healthy individuals to sell them. Despicable, but that's us *Homo sapiens*. When there is a market with a lot of money to be made, I'd be very surprised if no one services it.

The fact that White people were buying slaves to keep them as slaves instead of forcing otherwise free people into slavery lowers the ethical burden significantly. Just like I said, these rats were going to be dead soon anyway, whether I bought them or not. Those slaves were going to be slaves to someone, either to Africans, some other White person, or to you. What's the difference besides you feeling better about yourself? Either way the person will be a slave, so you're not helping them by abstaining.

Next comes the hopelessness. Poor redneck Whites who worked outside themselves weren't often buying slaves, but that doesn't mean that slave purchasers had infinite money. They may figure that they can't afford to buy slaves just to set them free. That would just cause the businesses that transported slaves across the Atlantic to bring more. They don't care what you do with them after you buy them; as long as you buy them the market exists. If they tried to steal the slaves to set them free, they'd just be criminals and go to prison. There is no easy way for them to help the slaves. In the end, it required fighting and winning a civil war.

After the hopeless impotence comes the wishful thinking. The slave owners could have convinced themselves that they would be better masters than the Africans, or the other White slave owners. They may plan to give them better living quarters, better work conditions, more time off, better food, and better health care. In some cases, they may have been right. They'd promise to do what a good Christian would, and read the Bible to them. Their slaves will recognize Jesus Christ as their Savior. Their lives wouldn't be great, but they'll be welcome in the kingdom of heaven after they die; that's what really matters, right? It may sound like I'm being facetious, but I do sincerely believe these could have been arguments slave purchasers made to justify their actions.

Finally, the real reason they're buying the slave. They have a snake, I mean family to take care of. Money. Slavery was much more common in the South than it was in the North. Is it because the Whites of the South were evil, and the Whites of the North were saints? I don't think so. I think it was because the Southern land and climate made agriculture a driving economic force in a way that wasn't applicable in the North. In other words, slaves were more economically useful in the South than they were in the North.

A similar argument could be made for why it was West Africans who captured their own people to sell to foreign slavers. Was it because Western Africans were uniquely immoral? I'd bet it was because it was easier to transport slaves to the New World from the west coast of Africa than Central or Eastern Africa. As you can see, the geographical context can be quite influential.

So they decide to buy the slaves. Are they going to mate with them? Suppose you told the average man that he owns a woman who has to do whatever he says for the rest of her life. You think he's not going to say something sexual? It's probably the first thing on his mind. If that's off the table, he might even give her back.

Even if the man is married, what percentage of married men would remain faithful their entire lives while owning other women? My guess is at least 20% of married men would cheat on their wives with one or more of their slaves. Do I know the precise number? No. I do know that American Black people aren't the same as Africans. Practically all of us have some White in our ancestry that occurred after our African ancestors were brought over.

This is a sensitive topic, so I want to clarify the point I'm trying to make here. It's easy for someone not reading closely to get confused and think I'm arguing that slavery is good or acceptable. Slavery is horrible. Slavery is disgusting. It's bad character to make sexual advances on someone under duress. These are all terrible things. I'd kill someone if they were trying to enslave me, if I could.

Does this make the people who committed these atrocities terrible people? I don't care how you answer that question. If the answer is yes, then we're all terrible people. Just terrible people in a better context, so you don't get to find out how terrible we are. If the answer is no, then you understand that regular people can do terrible things in bad contexts. Both perspectives are practically identical.

Multivariate Societal Contexts

The real world is a complicated place. A good indicator of understanding something is being able to predict it. Even relatively simple problems like predicting a person's sprinting speed can require quite a few variables to understand.

Suppose you're tasked with predicting how fast a student can run based on height alone, a single variable. You have twenty-five high school students' heights, and you know how long it took each of them to sprint one hundred meters. You transform their times into a speed in kilometers per hour. If you plot the students' heights on the x axis of the graph, and their speeds on the y axis, you will likely notice that height is positively correlated with speed. That is, taller students will tend to have higher speeds than shorter students.

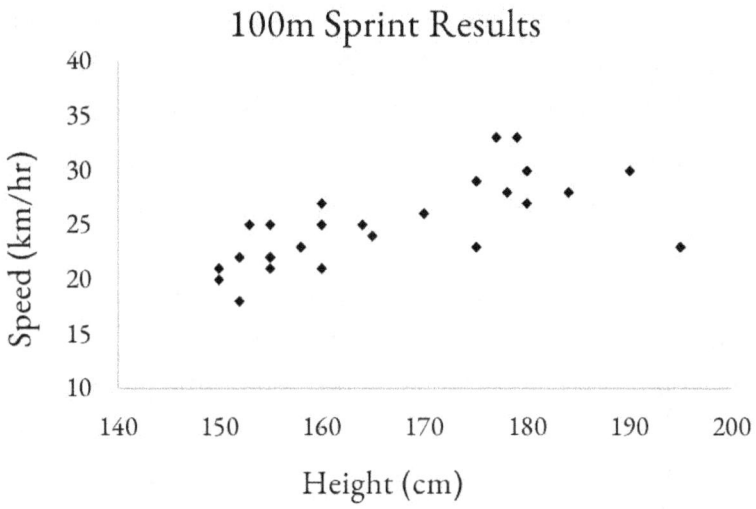

If you're a thinking person, you know that height alone is far from the whole story. What about the students' weights? Surely obese students would be slower than the average student. Why look at height specifically? If the stride is important, would the length of one's legs be a better predictor than height? How about if we knew each student's sports activities? I'd bet that students on the track team would be faster on average than students on the wrestling team, which would be faster than students who don't play any sports.

If we knew their grade point averages, could that tell us anything? Maybe students with very high or low GPAs would end up running slower times. Should we consider their biological sex? Perhaps seniors will be faster than freshmen on average, so let's consider their age. All of these questions introduce new variables into the equation of predicting a student's speed.

Considering all of the variables, sometimes called *factors*, above, should help us predict a student's speed with much greater accuracy than we could with height alone. Sarah is 165 centimeters tall, and Jane is 168. With a single variable, height, we would predict that Jane is faster, since there is a positive correlation between height and speed. As we consider additional factors, we learn that Sarah is on the track team and Jane isn't on any teams. With this new information, we're likely to change our minds, and predict that Sarah will be faster instead.

As we discussed all the variables, you may have had the intuition that some of them would be better predictors of speed than others. For instance, you may think that a student's sports activities or their weight will be better at predicting their speed than their GPA. Let's go a step further and suppose we considered hair color as a variable. Hair color will likely have very little predictive validity. GPA may be a little better than hair color, and sports activity may be the best predictor. Suppose we had the results of a sprint they did three months ago. That would probably be an even better predictor, since the fastest and slowest people three months ago are likely still the fastest and slowest today.

Statisticians, academics, and scientists run analyses similar to what we've discussed above all the time. This is because it's a good objective way to prove your claims based on data. You think z thing happens for y reason? Perform the statistics with real data and see if *y* actually predicts *z*. A more precise explanation is to prove with statistics *how well y* predicts *z*.

The question of *how well* can be answered with numbers. Specifically, the variable *r* represents the *coefficient of correlation*, which basically explains how things move together. The value of *r* can be between –1 and 1. If *r* is –1, that means the two things are perfectly inversely correlated. An example could be the percentage of empty volume in a cup predicting the percentage of full volume in a cup as liquid is poured in or out. As empty volume goes up, full volume goes down, and vice versa. An *r* near 0 means the things aren't correlated much at all, like speeds and hair color.

In order to determine how much of an outcome can be explained by the variables in our analysis, we use something called the *coefficient of determination*, which is r^2. The sign of *r* doesn't matter. We can predict things just as well with correlations (*r*) near –1, as correlations near 1. The predictive power of a variable diminishes as *r* approaches 0.

Squaring *r* causes us to end up with a positive number between 0 and 1. This number is the percentage of the variability of the outcome that we can explain or predict simply by knowing the values of our factors. In short, it tells us how much of the story our variables can explain. If we end up with an r^2 of 0.36, it indicates that *r*, the correlation, is either 0.6 or –0.6. An r^2 of 0.36 means that the variables we're using can only explain 36% of the variance of the outcome. This means most of the story, 64%, is unknown, and we need better variables. However, if we have an r^2 north of 0.98, it looks like we have most of it figured out.

Let's practice with a real political example. Some conservatives think that lowering tax rates increases tax revenue. Their argument is that cutting taxes increases GDP, so much so that the government will collect more in taxes even at a lower rate. Instead of calling them foolish, we can use statistics to determine if their argument is supported by the data.

Imagine we picked some thirty-year time period and found the correlation, r, between the federal income tax rate and GDP growth. If conservatives are right, we'd expect r to be negative. That would mean that as tax rates are decreased, GDP growth increases, and vice versa.

Assume we calculate the real r value and it ends up being near 0. This would mean that there is no strong correlation between tax rates and GDP growth. This finding would counter the conservative argument that cutting taxes increases tax revenue due to an increase in GDP.

Before we begin celebrating, I'm sure our conservative friends would have some objections. We only looked at federal income taxes, what about corporate taxes, municipal taxes, capital gains taxes, and estate taxes? What if tax cuts happened more often when unemployment was high? That could mean poor GDP growth during years when taxes were low wasn't because of low taxes, but because of the unemployment rate.

What our conservative friends are saying above is something like, "Let's not just look at height to determine speed, let's bring in more variables." This is a valid criticism. However, once you start to move in this direction, you can use statistical wizardry to end up with results that support whatever narrative you want to sell. All you have to do is selectively choose which variables to include, and cherry-pick the time period. You can do this quite easily if the people you're trying to convince don't know statistics. It's even easier if they share your political views, and want to believe what you're selling them in the first place.

Apologies for dragging you through some quantitative analytics you may have found less than exhilarating. If you're an oddball like me who actually enjoys those kinds of analyses, I'd encourage you to look up simple linear and multiple linear regressions. For everyone else, though it may not have been enjoyable, I am of the opinion that basic statistics are valuable for people to understand. Perhaps more high schools should teach it.

Understanding the contexts that lead to societies we would describe as "good" or "bad" requires a lot of variables. Far more than the number of variables needed to predict how fast someone is, or how tax rates impact tax revenues. This is a big problem to attempt to understand, let alone solve. Understanding statistics won't magically give us the answer, but it does give us a framework from which to think about multivariate problems, which most political issues are.

Empiricism and Rationalism

Not all societies are created equal. Some are highly conducive to human happiness, and some aren't. What's the difference? Determining the quality of a society is a multivariate problem with many factors to consider. It's practically impossible to solve, because people won't always agree on what a "good" society looks like. Regardless of whether or not this question can be solved objectively, it can be analyzed logically like a statistics problem. The objective is to understand each significant societal factor, and whether it correlates positively or negatively with creating a society we'd like to live in. See a non-exhaustive list of factors below.

- **External factors**
  - Geography (natural resources on your land, access to ports and waterways, climate, etc.)
  - Wealth level compared to other societies
  - Military strength compared to other societies
  - Presence or absence of aggressive neighbors
  - Diplomatic relationships with other nations
  - Level of global interconnectivity in this time period
  - Ability to attract international talent

- **Governance factors**
  - Type of government (democracy, monarchy, dictatorship, etc.)
  - Economic system
  - Legal system
  - Shapes of wealth and income distribution
  - Presence or absence of a state religion
  - Level of religious tolerance
  - Stance on individual rights
  - Stance on gender equality
  - Education systems
  - Immigration policy
  - Social programs
  - Level of freedom of speech
  - Cleanliness and infrastructure
  - Level of corruption

- **Citizenry factors**
  - Work ethic
  - Interest in education

- Rate of single parenthood
- Ethnic diversity
- Population level, average age, and density
- Level of xenophobia
- Crime rate
- Level of disease resistance
- Religion

Each factor above could be explored in depth by historians and political scientists who are much better equipped than I am. I'm sure there are plenty of relevant factors that aren't included above. Due to the scope, we won't be digesting everything here. Most of the external factors are difficult to change. The governance factors are where most political discourse is concentrated.

Here, I'd like to focus on the citizenry. This is where culture expresses itself. Cultural changes can be extremely impactful. In democracies like ours, they can also influence governance factors. The term *culture war* is used to describe one of the driving forces of tribalism in the United States. Before we do a deep dive into the citizenry, we'll take a detour to discuss the difference between *empiricism* and *rationalism*. Understanding the distinction between these terms will be helpful as we explore the bounds of cultural expression in human societies.

Rational. Empirical. Both sound like academic, sciencey words. What's the difference between them? Empiricism is more scientific. Rationalism is more intellectual or philosophical. Something is true empirically if it is supported by verifiable experiments. We don't have to understand why something is empirically true for it to be empirically true. Rationalism is using logic to understand how things work or make arguments. I'll give a few examples. The first will be the story of Dr. Ignaz Semmelweis.

In 1846, Dr. Semmelweis worked in a hospital with two different maternity wards. One was staffed by doctors and medical students. The other was staffed by female midwives. He discovered that women were five times more likely to die in the clinic staffed with doctors and medical students than in the clinic staffed with midwives. He wanted to find out what was causing such a drastic difference in the fatality rates. Were midwives simply better at delivering children than doctors? He had no idea, so he tried multiple different experiments.

The midwives typically had women give birth on their sides. The doctors had them give birth on their backs. Semmelweis instructed the doctors to try having women give birth on their sides like the midwives did. This had no effect on reducing the fatality rate.

In the doctor's clinic, whenever a woman died, a priest would walk through the halls ringing a bell. He figured that this bell could be scaring the women, which caused an internal reaction that made them more likely to have complications. He asked the priest to stop ringing the bell. It also had no effect. Looking at the empirical statistics, the factors of birth position and bell sounds had correlations (r) near 0 with the fatality rate.

He thought about the doctors' other activities and noticed that they often worked with dead bodies doing autopsies. He hypothesized that there could be small parts of the corpses they were working with that got into the women's bodies, causing them to get sick and die. So, he asked doctors to wash their hands and disinfect their tools with chlorine before working with the women. At last, the fatality rate in the doctors' ward began to decline precipitously. Cleaning their hands and tools had a strongly negative correlation with the fatality rate. Clean your equipment, and the fatality rate goes down. Fail to clean, and the rate goes up.

Washing hands and disinfecting tools worked empirically. Rationally, scientists at the time, and Semmelweis himself, had no knowledge of germs. He didn't know that the "pieces of corpse" he was concerned about were bacteria or viruses, which were themselves forms of life. Rationally, he didn't understand the full story. Empirically, the problem was solved.

In 1916, through his understanding of physics, mathematics, and his own creative intuition, Albert Einstein predicted the existence of gravity waves that could ripple through space-time at the speed of light. Sure, it sounded reasonable, but we didn't know if it was actually true, since no one had detected them yet. One hundred years later in 2016, our detectors first picked up signs of these gravitational waves. Today, we use gravitational waves as well as light waves to analyze the cosmos. Einstein's ingenuity made the rationalistic case for gravity waves. We didn't find out that he was correct empirically until our detectors found them, and validated that they behaved as he predicted.

It's difficult to get empiricism and statistics wrong. All you have to do is watch what happens, record the results, and plug them into statistics equations. Rationalism is the realm of inquiry that tests the quality of our thinking. Given the broad range of our rationalistic capabilities, remaining in the realm of empiricism and statistics is usually a safer bet. Anyone can look through Galileo's telescope. Few of us can use original thought to predict new physics phenomena our machines will detect sometime next century.

Empiricism, statistics, and rationalism are not just tools for science. They are also used, in varying degrees, to create policy. People often lead with rationalistic arguments because we don't know the empirical data, we don't understand statistics, and we think the problem can be explained by one or two variables.

Even if a person is justifiably confident in their reasoning abilities, simply being unaware of a key fact can cause them to arrive at the wrong conclusion. Not by fault of bad logic, but of incomplete information. Since it's impossible to be sure we're not missing anything, it's wise to have an open mind on almost all topics.

Too often, political vitriol is created because closed-minded zealots on both sides are dreaming up imaginary utopias that wouldn't work even if they implemented their ideas. A single logical error or missing fact can shatter the validity of an entire worldview. This should make them fragile, but unfortunately, poor worldviews are remarkably resilient. This is largely due to closed-mindedness, bias, and wishful thinking. Instead of listening to valid criticism, zealots often just blame the opposition for the fact that we're not currently in their imaginary utopia. They preferred to put Galileo in prison than to look through his telescope and be forced to change their minds. *They* are *us*.

Let's get out of the realm of optimal utopias where everyone has an idea and most of them are bad. Instead, let's set the current reality as our base, and make small changes with the goal of making tomorrow better than today. Do this over a long enough period of time, and that's the most likely way to successfully arrive at something resembling utopia. In contrast to civilizations of the past, you could argue that we're already here.

If we ground conversations in empirical facts without doing it in a disrespectful, know-it-all way, we can establish some bounds of truth from which to have constructive discourse. Having the humility to allow our rational prowess to take a back seat to empirical data is a great way to open our minds and understand each other. Understanding each other has a correlation near -1 with tribalism.

What Can Normal Look Like?

Orville and Wilbur Wright are famous for being the first to invent, build, and fly a motor-operated airplane. Magnificent, kudos to them. Let's explore a hypothetical world where their parents decided not to have children. In this world, the Wright brothers didn't exist, so whoever would have been second to invent the airplane would now be the first. Let's call the new first people to invent the airplane, the Rong brothers.

There are a lot of details that go into a machine as large and intricate as an airplane. Would we expect the plane invented by the Rong brothers to be identical to the plane invented by the Wright brothers? Almost certainly not. Would we expect it to have wings? Almost certainly. The same goes for some hand-controlled system to navigate in three dimensions while airborne. Propellors and a lightweight engine would likely have been included too.

The fundamentals would overlap. The details of how those fundamentals are implemented could vary, like using a different material for the wings. Perhaps the engine the Rong brothers used would have been more powerful, but less efficient. The position of the hand controls relative to the pilot could have been different as well.

Fast-forward to the present day in the timeline of the Rong brothers. How different would modern airplanes look in the Rong brothers' timeline, compared to airplanes in our current timeline? I believe they would be almost identical. Why?

Products are refined over time in the marketplace in a process that could be compared to natural selection. First, customers receive a useful, but far from perfect product. The Wright brothers' first airplanes wouldn't fare well in competition with the fleet of Delta Air Lines. Their first planes weren't useful for travelling over an ocean, or even carrying multiple people. It was, however, something that worked a little bit. From there, the process of refinement begins. Customers complain about the product's imperfections, then the business fixes the problems, which improves the product. If the business doesn't listen to the customer, another company will. Then the process continues with the new company being the victor.

This is one of the many reasons why venture capital professionals who invest in start-ups care so much about the quality of the team. A good process beats a good idea in the long run almost every time. A good process will soon arrive at a good idea, and then continue improving upon it. A good idea often isn't as good as you think. Even when it is, you can get stuck, and lose to someone who turned your good idea into a better one. A strong team that is technically skilled and humble enough to act on customer feedback is well positioned for success.

The dumb empiricist can grind away at the natural advantage a smart rationalist has, if the rationalist is not also empirical. The ideal is a rational empiricist. I believe that airplanes of today would look nearly identical in the Wright and the Rong brothers' timelines, because of the power of empiricism. I don't think that the current airplane designs are due to the genius of rationalist engineers. I believe the current designs are based on the needs of customers.

Humans like comfortable seats. Humans like air conditioning. Humans sometimes need to use the restroom. Humans like having the option to order a drink or a small snack. We like being safe, so seat belts will end up existing. I don't think it matters in the long run who was the first to invent any of them. I can almost guarantee that if they didn't do it, there would have been a second first. Perhaps the Wright brothers are the Rong brothers after all, due to some other couple not having offspring interested in aviation.

What does my belief in the inevitability of modern plane design have to do with societal contexts? Earlier in this chapter, I listed some external, governmental, and citizenry factors whose values could positively or negatively correlate with how "ideal" a given society is. I also claimed that most people will be normal people, whatever "normal" is for the society they are born into. Are there limits on what "normal" can be for a society? We know that "normal" in one society and "normal" in another can be very different, but can it be anything? I'd argue no. Airplanes can have different types of lighting. They cannot decide against having an engine.

As we explore the bounds of what "normal" can be, think like an empiricist. Thinking like a rationalist is likely to introduce bias or morality into the discussion. These things are not relevant to what normal can possibly be. Before we begin, let's make a distinction between values that are more or less valid for a society's survival, and values that would make us more or less likely to want to live in that society.

If something helps or hurts a society's chance at survival, we'll call it *valid* or *invalid*. If something makes a society closer to or further from the ideal, we'll call it *good*, *bad*, *better*, or *worse*. For example, I don't like parasites. I think parasites are a bad form of life. Regardless of how I feel about them, empirically, parasites are a valid form of life.

Normal for a society has to be in some harmony with how humans work. It doesn't have to be a great match for human nature, but it can't be entirely destructive toward it. Technically it could, but your society would soon disappear, so that "normal" wouldn't exist very long. There is a lot of room to be horrible and still be within human nature, unfortunately.

For example, let's start with two hypothetical societal stances on sexuality. One where the society persecutes and kills homosexuals, and one where society persecutes and kills heterosexuals. We don't have to look hard through history, or even the present moment, to find societies where homosexual activity is a crime that is punishable by death. The murderous persecution of homosexuals is an extremely bad thing from my perspective. However, it is not invalid in relation to the survival of a society. In other words, it can be "normal" in a society.

In contrast, let's imagine a society where heterosexual activity is a crime that is punishable by death. Principally, an anti-heterosexual society is just as bad and immoral as an anti-homosexual society. However, I believe that heterosexual persecution is invalid for the survival of a society. I don't think it can be "normal" like homosexual persecution can.

What's the difference? There are many more heterosexual people than homosexual people generally, so you're more likely to have serious internal wars and bloodshed. Either the heterosexual majority will win, and of course won't continue those policies, or they will lose and your population will decline because there aren't enough children. It is possible for gay men and lesbian women to have babies technically. It's more likely now than before with modern science, but practically, it's not happening enough to sustain a society.

I don't believe heterosexual people are better than homosexual people. However, a society can attempt to purge homosexual people and still function as a bad society. A society that attempts to purge heterosexual people cannot function as a society at all. Both are equally bad, but one is valid, and the other is invalid. One can be normal. The other cannot.

Another invalid context is that of a society that supports murdering each other within the in-group at scale. You may think, people murder each other all the time, especially in violent cultures. This is true, but the vast majority of the time when people murder someone, they're murdering some *them*, not an *us*.

Killing *them* is an argument a lot of humans can get behind, or at least entertain. Killing *us*, is not. The difference is only bias most of the time of course, but being biased, unfortunately, is valid. Even if you could find a group of lunatics who form a group and enjoy murdering each other, that group probably isn't going to last long, so it's invalid by default.

Sure, policies that involve killing a majority of your population aren't very sustainable. What is the point? Thinking objectively about what normal can be is a prerequisite for understanding why many human societies have common characteristics. Why some characteristics are subject to change, and others are not. Understanding the bounds of human civilization allows us to understand the bounds of ourselves. This understanding should make it easier to respect a box that appears unworthy based on the ideas within it.

We began by discussing invalid options for societies. Next, we'll discuss less valid options that hurt a society's chance for survival without disqualifying it. Finally, we'll end with valid options that make societies more likely to survive. Sometimes there are conflicts between what we think is good, and what is actually valid. Often, we're uncertain what is valid, even if we can agree on what good is. This is why we have politics.

Let's consider a society that is very high in altruism. This society gives most of its excess resources to the neediest societies nearby. Many people would consider this society morally good. This behavior won't cause the society to fail to exist overnight, but it isn't very valid. A healthy amount of selfishness in a society is beneficial for survival. A society that gives away its resources without receiving a comparable benefit in return will end up poorer than it otherwise would have been, all else equal. This negatively contributes to the society's odds of survival. Of course, being so selfish that you alienate yourself until you have no allies is bad for survival as well. There is a balance to strike.

Envision a society that idolizes the Wild West, and adopts a "might makes right" attitude. In this society, it's up to each individual to defend themselves. The legal system is very lax; society is more lawless than lawful, and vigilantes are more common than police. Some people who think they are tough guys or have extreme distrust of the government may think this is a good context. I'd argue that it is not very valid.

If a government is easy on crime and encourages private citizens to handle themselves, this is more likely to create an environment full of criminal organizations. This will result in high levels of corruption and crime across the board. It will be hard to attract talent or international investment in this nation. Though some minority of people may prefer lawlessness, it negatively contributes to the survival of the society for social and economic reasons.

Not everything matters. Some factors will correlate positively with a society's survival. Some factors will correlate negatively with it. Some factors won't correlate with survival much at all. For example, consider two societies that both have forty-hour workweeks. One of them begins their two-day weekend on Friday, and the other begins theirs on Saturday. This is a difference, but which two days they have off of work won't significantly impact survival.

Sometimes the interest of a society may not be in the interest of humanity. This kind of situation is difficult to navigate. Climate change policy is a good example. It may be damaging to the validity of a society to limit its greenhouse gasses, since it is cheaper for it to use dirty energy. If the society spends its resources to protect the environment, it pays the cost, but the whole world receives the benefit. In economics, things like this are called *public goods*.

Public goods are *non-exclusionary* and *non-rivalrous*. Non-exclusionary means that you can't stop someone from using the good you paid for. Non-rivalrous means that as someone uses your good, it doesn't impact the ability of someone else to use it. For example, missile defense of an area is non-exclusionary because if the area is secure, people who didn't pay for it get protected too. You can't exclude them. It's non-rivalrous because one person being protected doesn't remove the protection from someone else.

No one has an incentive to pay for a public good in a free market. Logical actors would just wait for someone else to pay for it. Why would I pay for streetlights on our street when I could let you do it? You can't stop me from seeing the light. Me seeing the light doesn't make it any darker for you. Since no logical market participant would pay for it, it's the role of the government to tax everyone, and then build streetlights with everyone's contributions. This is how we eliminate the problems of *free riders* and dark streets.

If a society spends its money on expensive clean energy to mitigate climate change, the whole world benefits. We can't turn off the benefits for nations that keep pumping dirty energy into the atmosphere. As rational economic actors, every country is better off, at least in the medium term, continuing to use cheap dirty fossil fuels, and hoping that other countries pay the price to take care of the earth.

In this regard, it is valid for the society to use dirty energy. However, it's a bad strategy at the humanity-level context in the long run. Unfortunately, the solution presented by economists requires a government to address the *free rider* problem with taxes.

There is no government with the authority to address *free riders* at the level of nations. I hope that doesn't mean we'll all end up living in the dark.

We don't need to discuss in detail all of the obviously good things that positively contribute to a society's validity. Things like the presence of a military, a legal system, antitrust laws, and regulatory bodies for the safety of food and drugs are table stakes. We agree on most of the things that have a strong positive correlation to the ideal society. Since these things so obviously contribute to goodness and validity, it will be rare that a society is missing more than a few of them. These are like having seats, lights, and a restroom on an airplane. We've figured that out. Now we're in the process of fine-tuning our societies. Figuring out how to make flying cheaper, how to make the middle seat a better experience, lower the rate of lost luggage, and so on.

Each of the factors we think contributes to how ideal a society is can be represented by variables a–z. For example, factor w could be the top speed limit, and factor x could be drug legalization policy. We can organize the factors into three buckets.

- Factors that have a neutral correlation with the ideal society, so their values don't matter
  - Don't waste too much time and energy on these.

- Factor-value pairs that are near ideal, making us closer to the ideal society
  - If it's not broken, don't fix it.

- Factor-value pairs that are far from ideal, pushing us further from the ideal society

- These are the items that require our attention. We'll need to write new policies, or change existing ones to improve our society.

Suppose factor h is affirmative action in college admissions. There may be disagreement about it, but if h is only weakly correlated with how ideal a society is, it doesn't matter that much. Suppose factor g is the amount we spend on government science grants. It's possible for us to think the value of g is great, but not be aware that another value for g would be far better. Perhaps the amount we spend on science grants is good, but would be optimal if it were 40% higher.

It's possible for us to think that c is irrelevant because we have k and s. We decide to remove it. Later, we may end up paying a price because we didn't understand all the good things c was doing for us. Which of our policies is the appendix organ that can be safely removed without causing harm? We removed one kidney and were fine afterward. It should be OK to remove the other one then, right? Wrong. We have to be careful.

Imagine the ideal society with every value tuned optimally to maximize the well-being of its citizens. This society is as good as we possibly can get. It's not as good as possible; the fact that we are flawed humans limits it from being as good as possible. It is, however, as good as it could possibly be for us. Ignoring our flaws, and assuming we're better than we are, is just wishful thinking that can lead to bad decisions.

Start from this hypothetical society that is as good as possible for us, then change the value of one of the factors from perfection, to merely acceptable. Let's say we changed the optimal federal income tax rate from whatever perfect was, to something not wholly unreasonable, but significantly worse. This society would still be far better than any society in history. It's still good, but it would be perfect again if that one factor, the tax rate in this instance, were changed back. That's what we're trying to do, except we're not so close as to be one step away from perfection. Though we're further than one step from perfection, we're still far closer than Nazi Germany, or the United States was two hundred years ago.

This process of changing the values of factors to create the ideal society is tricky business. It can be like deciding to turn a particular side on a Rubik's cube. Even if the move seems right, you may not know that it is. After a few turns in the wrong direction, you could end up totally lost and unable to find your way back. Also, time moves on and contexts change. The objective end position of the cube may not remain keeping all sides one color.

Given that things change over time, we will need to make some decisions. Doing nothing is a decision, and even that one can be costly. We have to make joint decisions that affect all of us in a complex environment full of uncertainty. Making the wrong decisions can have significant, potentially life-or-death consequences. It's no wonder that politics is such a charged topic.

Religious Tolerance

During our discussion of societal factors, I intentionally left out a big one—religion. It's influential enough to be worthy of its own discussion. In the United States, there is a separation between church and state. However, there is no separation between church and politics. Religious disagreements are a common source of political tension; this is true sometimes even between individuals of the same faith who interpret doctrine differently.

Religion is literature. Literature is art. Beauty is in the eye of the beholder. That's the problem. The subjective nature of religion makes it difficult to agree on. Religion is important and subjective. How do we deal with something like that? With empiricism, and caution.

This is going to be a discussion about whether religion *generally* has a positive or negative correlation with how ideal a society is. To answer this question, we'll perform an empirical analysis of the historical impact all religions have had on their societies. Human memory is short. So short, that we often think about religion as a choice between Judaism, Islam, and Christianity. Religion as a concept is so big that it can be broken down into categories.

There are monotheistic religions, polytheistic religions, new religions like Mormonism, popular religions of today like Islam or Christianity, Eastern religions like Hinduism or Buddhism, old religions rarely practiced today like Zoroastrianism and Mithraism, the religious beliefs of ancient South American tribes, and so on. Not to mention all the other religions we aren't aware of since humans began walking the earth in our current form over three hundred thousand years ago.

All of those examples are in the same bucket of "religions" for the sake of this empirical discussion. This is the only objective way I could think of to talk about it. This way it doesn't matter if you're a Christian, Muslim, or an atheist. It doesn't matter if you think a particular religious claim is true or hogwash. We can discuss religion generally with respect to its impact on societies.

Since we're talking about all religions, by default everyone should be able to agree that practically all of them are wrong. By wrong, I mean that they are not literally true descriptions of how our universe works. If religions are distinct, and one is right, all the others are wrong. At best, one is right. If you're religious, we can continue this discussion assuming whatever your religion is, is the one that's literally true. If you're an atheist, assume all of them are false. These positions are almost entirely the same, except one.

There are likely religions numbering in the thousands over the three hundred thousand years humans have been on the planet. Even if you think "thousands" is too high, there have been at the very least one hundred. Many of them would have been small folk religions that were nowhere near as large as religions of today; they served a societal purpose nonetheless.

The first empirical truth to account for is that the vast majority of societies in human history will have believed in a religion that is not literally true. Given that a maximum of one religion is true out of hundreds or thousands throughout human history, you can't argue otherwise. Most modern religions of today have been around less than three thousand years. That's about 1% of the time humans have been on earth. If one of the right religions was made in the last three thousand years, every society for 99% of human history had to have had the wrong religion.

We've established that all religions, except yours, are wrong. This means all religious texts and traditions, except the ones related to yours, were made up by regular people. What this tells me, is that there is something about us as humans that causes us to make up religions on an ongoing basis.

Scientology, Mormonism, and Jehovah's Witnesses are all younger than the United States. In 1990, a man named Ahmad Mushaddeq claimed to be the next prophet of Islam, and has garnered over fifty thousand followers. We also know that religions can be remarkably stable in a society despite the fact that they are wrong. A religion being wrong does not render the society it exists within invalid for survival, that's for sure. So, we have religions, and the consequences for them being wrong aren't destructive for their societies. Untrue religions are still valid.

Let's assume, even the atheists reading this, that there is one correct religion, and we know which one it is. Does that mean that all of the other religions in the history of human societies have been worthless? Is it a strictly bad thing for a society to believe in a religion that isn't literally true? Is it possible that despite being wrong, a religion could have a positive correlation with creating an ideal society?

Religion is almost omnipresent in the history of human societies. It's like looking at the leaves of many kinds of trees around the world, and noticing that the vast majority of them are green. Suppose that we don't know about photosynthesis or chlorophyll. We wouldn't understand what the leaves were doing aside from providing shade. We may have thought that being green was arbitrary. Yet without the green, without the chlorophyll, the trees would die.

I'm not arguing that an untrue religion is as valuable to human societies as chlorophyll is to trees. I'm arguing that we're dealing with something empirically abundant that we don't fully understand rationalistically. At least I don't. Many religious people and atheists would agree that it's a strictly positive thing to remove an untrue religion from a society. It's possible that it would be, but I don't think we have enough information to be sure.

We discussed what normal can be for a society. How about what normal can be for a religion? Any religion that influences the culture in such a way that results in an invalid society for survival, would be invalid as a religion as well. Beyond this low bar, it's just like anything else. A successful untrue religion has to work with human nature, which can be quite terrible, but within certain limits.

Religions will be more successful if people want to believe in them. Wanting to believe in something doesn't make it true, but it makes it much easier to sell. A good positive story that tells you your family is still alive after death, whether it's via heaven, reincarnation, or the like, is an attractive product. It's certainly more attractive than one that tells you you're going to hell in the end, no matter what you do. Since it's easier to sell, untrue religions are generally going to be positive with their messaging.

Untrue religions that are too grounded in short-term predictions won't last very long. Suppose a religion claims that in two years, the sun will enter an eclipse lasting one thousand years while their sun god is being reborn. Most of the religion is based on that one-thousand-year eclipse. This religion could last a maximum of two years. Since its predictions are so specific, and so short term, it will rapidly lose credibility and disappear. This means that for untrue religions to last, they must have core tenets that are based on unfalsifiable claims. If they were falsifiable, they would be falsified. For any claims they do make, it is beneficial for there to be some mysticism or "mysterious ways" to serve as an insurance policy for anything the writers of the untrue religion may have omitted, or gotten wrong.

We don't need to keep discussing specific examples. Continue the above analysis for what "normal" can be for a religion, and you'll see why religions around the world today, and in human history, have so many similarities. The golden rule is like airplanes having seats and a restroom. It's not a conspiracy. It doesn't mean all religions are true. It means the customers, *Homo sapiens*, like it. Since we like it, successful untrue religions will have some form of it. The ones that don't, will go out of business.

Now we understand why untrue religions often look similar:

because they're serving the same customers. Back to the question of whether an untrue religion is good or bad for society. Looking at history, it's not hard to find examples of bad things being done in the name of untrue religions. Child sacrifices, burning women at the stake, persecution of homosexuals, and so on. Clearly, there can be bad consequences for untrue religious beliefs.

How about the good side? I like Christmas; it's the most wonderful time of the year. I know people who have turned their lives around for the better because of religion. I know religious organizations that regularly bring communities together, and make efforts to support the needy in society. Has the net impact of untrue religions been positive or negative in human history? I certainly didn't cover all the positives and negatives in this chapter. I couldn't in an entire book.

My purpose for analyzing untrue religions in this section isn't to tell you I know the answers. Quite the contrary. I don't know the answers. There is at least a possibility that an untrue religion is good for a person or a society. Instead of having conflicts with people who have different religious beliefs than us, judging them or attacking them, consider that they may have just needed something and now they have it.

Don't read this paragraph if you're a sensitive person, you've been warned. Anecdotally, when I was a teenager, one of my sports coaches told us he used to bury cats up to their necks in the dirt and run their heads over with a lawn mower. He told us he stopped doing it because he found Jesus. Whether or not Christianity is the one true religion, this man needed Jesus, and I'm glad he has him.

As we near the conclusion of our discussion about contexts, I'd like to bring the bots from chapter 3 back into the conversation. We've established that most people will be normal people, whatever "normal" means for the society they are born into. This is similar to saying that most people will be bots. Almost all of us have some incorrect bot-beliefs that we don't know about. Even the least bot-like individuals often still have some influences from the default beliefs they were indoctrinated with.

Imagine bots are made of cookie dough. Culture, of which religion is a factor, is the shape of the scoop. Culture creates the blueprint prototypical person the bots are molded from. Individuals will change over time to varying degrees, but culture provides the prototype that we start out with. With respect to the box analogy from chapter 2, culture is like an instruction manual of best practices that comes with the box.

The measure of a successful culture is how well it sets its bots up for success. It should start the bots out on the right foot, so to speak. You can't expect the bots to think for themselves, on average. Even when they do, you can't rely on them to have good ideas. It's helpful to start off with a good instruction manual in the box. This way we don't need to reinvent wisdom over and over again. We can ignore the instructions we don't feel are necessary, at our own risk.

I'd like to end with an analogy related to the highest context, above societal. This is an analogy that musically inclined people like me may especially appreciate. While listening to music, a certain note may sound eerie. Musical scores for horror films often have disturbing music that makes your hair stand up. Take one of those particularly creepy sounding notes, for example. Someone untrained in music theory may understandably think that's the "creepy note." It's scary. They don't trust it. It makes them feel the need to look over their shoulder.

They may have the intuition that whenever that note is played, it will sound creepy. It certainly feels that way while you're hearing the note in the context of the notes that came before it. It makes sense not to be able to fathom that note sounding anything but creepy in your current context. However, someone with a basic understanding of music theory will know that all notes are practically the same. Any of them could "feel" any way depending on the context they are played in. That same creepy note that listeners don't trust could be bright and vibrant in a different song. It can be difficult even for musicians to think in a different context while experiencing the current one.

Humans are like that note. Depending on the context, our note could feel any of the full range of human emotions. The question is, what song are we listening to? We could listen to some death metal or aggressive hip-hop and attune ourselves to a rhythm of war. We could listen to gospel and feel the Holy Spirit. We could listen to jazz and ponder the meaning of life.

Metaphorically speaking, we have a demon on our left shoulder, an angel on our right shoulder, and a light bulb above our head. Good music that aligns with the human condition is coming from all three directions, even from the demon.

I prefer to look up. I respect looking right, and I respect the people looking left, even though I don't respect their decision. If you want someone to change their tune, don't tell them their music sucks. Invite them to enjoy your music with you. If they listen, it might just throw off their rhythm from the context they were in. If they end up liking your song, they may have a hard time understanding how they haven't been listening to it all along.

7. Being Wrong Has Consequences

"It's easier to fool people than it is to convince them that they have been fooled."
— Mark Twain

♩ I Can't Get Started I Oscar Peterson

If people could know better, they would. There is a certain lack of freedom that comes with understanding something. You're free to lie about what you believe. You can try to stop thinking about it. Yet once you truly understand something, you can't go back. This could be the cause of the old adage, "Great minds think alike." This is generally true, and it's not by mistake. If you're going to be wrong about something, you usually have a near infinite number of options to choose from. There is great diversity among bad ideas. On the other hand, if you're going to be right about something, you usually only have a few options at best. Often only one.

The chains that understanding binds us with are powerful. Simply by making sense, we can force others to agree with us, and it works both ways. Are you free to believe that 2+2 = 3? You couldn't believe it if your life depended on it. You could say it, but you couldn't believe it because you understand addition, hopefully.

This means that if we make sense and our opposition hears us, they will have no choice but to agree. It's harder than it sounds, because it requires sharing a fundamental goal, and targeting the root of disagreement, as opposed to the branches. Forcing someone to change their mind with reason alone is difficult. Remember, everything goes down easier with a side of good faith.

Though many approach the art of persuasion as an intellectual dominance game, I recommend against it. Thinking of it like a game often makes you afraid to lose, and you become rigid. You being rigid makes your conversation partner rigid. If your opponent feels like they're engaged in an intellectual battle, one thing they know for sure is that they can't let you win. In short, if it feels like a battle, you're losing the battle.

The best way to get your conversation partner to be willing to change their mind is by showing that you're willing to change yours. Take the lead by stepping into a vulnerable position, and they may follow. Push, and they're probably going to push back harder. Instead of being opponents in a game, be comrades looking for valuable insights together. They don't want *you* to win. *Us* winning, however, isn't so bad.

Changing someone's mind about something important is one of the best gifts you can give a person. Gaining a new perspective on a topic you care about. Noticing connections you didn't see before, as things begin to "click" in your mind. It doesn't often come with a "thank you," but it is well deserved.

Social media is filled with clips claiming that someone on one side "owned" someone on the other side. How often does the "owned" person change their mind? Those videos are often outlets for people already on the same side to pat each other on the back about how great they are compared to their foolish enemies. Useless, and shallow.

The consequences of being wrong can be severe. One of the

worst consequences is when being wrong makes others dislike you so much, they lose interest in helping you become right. Imagine that every time we got a math question wrong, it caused our teacher to hate us, and refuse to teach us any more mathematics. We're not great at math now, but we'd be much worse. It's a bad idea for mathematics, and it's a bad idea for politics. If someone is wrong about immigration or social justice issues, don't hate them, help them. To help them you shouldn't be an opponent, you should be a comrade.

From Fear to Hatred

Pathos is king when it comes to inspiring action. It's what gets us out of bed in the morning. *Logos* tells us the specific steps to take, and *ethos* tells us who we should trust. I don't believe most political influencers and advertisers are aware of Greek rhetorical terms. In any case, you don't need to know how a toilet works in order to use it. Emotion motivates and, unfortunately, fear is one of the easiest emotions to generate. Nostalgia and disgust can be dangerous as well, especially when combined.

It's not often that we like things we're afraid of. If someone can convince us to be afraid of a group of people, odds are we aren't going to like those people. Over time, this can lead to hatred. Even if the fears are unfounded, based on hypothetical futures that will never exist, the fear itself is real, and it has real consequences.

Let's discuss an example of how fear can lead to racism. Without knowing the actual statistics, most of us would assume that Black people commit violent crimes at a higher rate than White people. If you think that, you are correct. As a teenager, Brad learned this was true statistically. Initially, he was nervous around Black people and didn't trust them. Over time, he came to simply not like Black people generally. While it's true that the Black violent crime rate is higher than the White violent crime rate, no two populations are going to have the *exact* same value for any continuous metric. We won't have the same exact average height, eyebrow width, hair thickness, rate of higher education, bone density, etc.

I know almost certainly that White people with brown eyes and White people with blue eyes commit crimes at a rate that isn't *exactly* the same. I don't know which is higher, but let's assume White people with brown eyes commit crimes at a higher rate than White people with blue eyes. Someone could take this kernel of truth and use it to build a rift between brown- and blue-eyed White people. People will start to believe that eye color is the difference that explains why some White people are more violent than others.

This is clearly foolish right? What about the Nazi "pure" blond-haired blue-eyed Aryan race? Few things are too foolish for us humans to believe. "Size matters" is a common response from those still looking to hold on to their hatred. I agree. The violent crime rates for the two groups of White people aren't exactly the same, but if they're close enough, the distinction may not matter, right? Well, how close is close enough? How different does the violent crime rate need to be to warrant treating people differently? Let's look at some real violent crime data from the FBI.

United States violent crime rates by race in 2016:

- Asian: 0.03%
- White: 0.12%
- Black: 0.36%

"Aha!" goes Brad, the racist conservative. "Black people are three times as likely as White people to commit violent crime."

True. White people are four times as likely Asian people to commit violent crime. Should Asians look at Whites the same way racist Whites look at Blacks? Based on the data, they should. For my racist White friends, you may want to look in the mirror and think twice before calling someone else the N-word.

How about we zoom out here and realize that all of these violent crime rates are less than half of 1%. Assume you interact with 100 Asian people, 100 Black people, and 100 White people. In each case, less than 1% of them will commit a violent crime this year. Due to how probabilities work, there is a chance that you get unlucky, and of the 100 White people you meet, 50 of them are violent criminals. However, the most likely number of violent criminals out of 100 for each race is 0. The second most likely number is 1, and the odds decline precipitously after that from 2 to 100. If you're interested in learning how to calculate the actual probabilities for finding x number of criminals out of 100 given the rates above, look up binomial statistics.

We've established that regardless of race, there is a good chance that 0 out of 100 people will be a concern to you. Assuming you do meet someone in the less than 1% who commits a violent crime in a given year; it's important to note that they see a lot of people every year. The odds that they are a danger to you specifically are much lower than the general violent crime rates above.

Is it bad that the Black violent crime rate is three times as high as the White one? Yes, it is. We should get better. However, even saying something like the "Black community" needs to reduce crime misleads people into thinking that the "Black community" is a criminal community. Again, the fact is that for all three races we covered, it's less than half of 1%.

Yes, size does matter, but is the difference between brown- and blue-eyed White people large enough to treat them differently? How about between Asians and Whites with a 4x difference? Between Whites and Blacks with a 3x difference? Between Blacks and Asians with a 12x difference?

You could state the truth that the Black crime rate is twelve times higher than the Asian crime rate, and good-intentioned people could walk away questioning whether or not we're the same species. If instead, you look at the total percentage likelihood of violent criminal behavior, Asians and Blacks differ by only a third of a percent. Humans do this all the time. We'll be 99% the same, find a difference in that 1%, and at the end of a long process it ends up being a reason to kill each other.

An implicit assumption of this analysis is that differences in race can explain the differences in crime rates. However, this is a single-variable analysis, which is cause for concern and skepticism. Suppose race can explain 30% of the differences in the violent crime rate. An analysis broken down by culture could sort Whites, Blacks, and Asians into buckets of stereotypical White, Black, and Asian culture. Might it be possible that this cultural analysis would be a better indicator than the racial analysis, explaining 35% of the differences?

Perhaps part of the reason the Asian crime rate is so low, is because a comparatively high percentage of Asians in the United States are first- or second-generation immigrants. These immigrants often arrive here on a work or education visa, which implies that they are some combination of ambitious and educated. Being ambitious and educated likely has a negative correlation with criminality. I wouldn't be surprised if Asians who stayed in Asia have a higher crime rate than Asians who recently immigrated to the United States.

Much of politics is people trying to solve complex problems while missing important variables. It's even worse when knowing some statistical truths gives them false confidence. The stats they know may only have a coefficient of determination (r^2) of 0.3 as it relates to solving the problem. Despite not even understanding a third of the story, they feel like experts, and then proceed to stop listening.

So here goes Brad, armed with the truth that Blacks are three times as likely as Whites to commit violent crimes. In Brad's mind, however bad Whites are, Blacks are three times worse. Three times more savage. He doesn't understand evolution, but he figures Black people must be behind in the process. He carries this attitude with him, and looks at all the Black people he sees with contempt. He looks down his nose at the scum infesting his country.

Brad saw thirty Black people this week. Despite his worldview, but in line with the statistics he only partially understands, none of them were criminals. He looked at all of them like they were. His fears aren't real, at least not at the scale he fears them. How he interacted with those thirty Black people, however, that's real. They could feel his disrespect and disdain for them. The "you don't belong here" look in his eyes.

How do you think they feel about Brad? Would you be surprised if some of them generalized their disdain for Brad onto White people as a whole? This is how the cycle of hatred perpetuates itself. Brad didn't start with hatred. He started with fear and distrust, which quickly turned into hatred. When this hatred is reciprocated by Black people, some innocent White person may be the victim of it. You know what comes next. We have to stop this.

How? By quoting some facts at Brad? Teaching Brad statistics? Proving to him that we can be three times different and still be 99%

the same? Using *logos* to convince him that his fears are unreasonable? We could try, but showing him that his fears are unreasonable is much better. Inviting him to the barbecue would probably be the best solution. Calling him a racist is only going to make the problem worse.

Democrats can use fear too. Republicans' success at overturning Roe v. Wade makes it easier for Democrats to win elections going forward, because now we can play the fear card. If Republicans win, they can try to ban abortions nationally. This is a good card for us to use, and we should use it. Still, I am nervous about ending up in a fear generation competition where fear turns to hatred and pulls us apart.

Generalizing the Individual

Like many of you, I've seen stupidity at levels that were quite impressive. Downright comical. Unbelievable. I'm not talking about people who were mentally impaired. I'm talking about perfectly healthy adults with impregnable foolishness. Often, these were highly successful people. Sometimes well-educated people. How can this be?

One piece of advice that has served me well, is to assume everyone is average intelligence until proven otherwise. The person is on TV in a suit? Average. The person is a millionaire business leader? Average. The person is a janitor? Average. The person is homeless? Average. The person is a child in an inner-city school? Average.

Some people are smarter than others for sure, and there are factors that are positively correlated with intelligence. However, guessing who is intelligent and who isn't based strictly on their level of monetary success is a mistake I fear is built into human nature. It's a results-oriented positive or negative ethos influencer that makes us inclined to listen to some people more than others. Being inclined to agree or disagree with someone is usually a bad thing. It distracts us from the *logos* of what they are saying, which should be the only thing that matters.

Suppose a five-year-old with an intellectual disability tells you that cryptocurrencies are risky investments. Then Mark Cuban tells you the same thing. It shouldn't matter who told it to you. Unfortunately, many people will write off the child by default. Those same people will often give billionaires like Cuban the benefit of the doubt, even if he were to say something that didn't make sense to them. Assume everyone is average, and you won't be biased toward getting conned by a successful con man. You also won't underestimate people based on what you think a smart person looks like.

I'd like to introduce a concept I call *generalizing the individual.* Most of us who were raised well know that it's bad to judge someone based on their skin color. Just because we've seen Black people do crime doesn't mean the Black person in front of us is a criminal. Just because I knew someone of a given profession who was corrupt, doesn't mean everyone of that profession is corrupt. This is common knowledge we all should understand.

What if I know someone individually is a criminal? In this case, people often feel comfortable generalizing the whole person as being a criminal. This is a mistake. For example, let's say someone has a violent criminal history and they admit guilt. This person is a criminal. But *is* he a criminal? No, he is a person who committed some specific crimes.

If we generalize and define his identity as "criminal," we could be biased to believe he did all kinds of things. Suppose he's a suspect for sexually abusing a child. If you define him *as* a criminal, you may jump to the conclusion that he's guilty. He's a criminal, criminals are guilty. Being a criminal is part of his identity, but it is not his whole identity; it may not even be a majority of it. In prison, many violent criminals despise and murder other inmates who are there for abusing children.

Let's take someone you know is stupid. You've talked to them before and they made negative logical sense. A complete imbecile, you think. Is this person stupid? He was in the experience you had with him. Though if you generalize "stupid" onto his whole identity, you're less likely to listen to what he's saying on another topic where he may actually make sense. In his next sentence, he may say something that would benefit you to learn. It would be a shame not to learn it because you generalized "stupid" onto his whole identity. Be careful when painting others as imbeciles, you just might spill some paint on yourself.

I define "good faith" as sincere positivity. Generalizing mental inferiority onto someone is at best, polite disrespect. When dealing with a force as powerful as tribalism, that's not good enough.

Tryouts for the Math Team

Do you remember those multistep math problems where your answer from part a is used as the input to part b, and then your answer from part b is the input for part c, and so on? If you had a good math teacher, they didn't penalize you for getting parts b and c wrong because you got part a wrong. If you logically implemented the processes correctly for parts b and c, you should get full credit for them, regardless of your input from part a. That's how a good math teacher grades assignments.

The universe, however, is not a good math teacher. In the real world, if you get part *a* wrong, you're not getting any points for *b* and *c*. The real world is strictly outcome oriented. It doesn't care about how hard you worked. It doesn't care how smart you are. There is no guarantee of fairness or justice.

Imagine someone takes a foolishly risky financial position. Nine out of ten people who take this type of risk lose most of their money; one in ten makes a ton of money. The one in ten who got lucky, let's call him Matthew, will be successful. Matthew has a nice house, an expensive car, and a beautiful partner at his side. He has confidence in himself because he thinks he understands something others don't. People will be inclined to believe him because, well, Matthew is very successful, and they are not.

I'd like to recount another tale starring John from my leadership class. Despite being in a master's program for finance, John had no business background. You should not ask John to solve problems involving numbers. However, he was very good with people. He was social, and he "played the game" very well. I always believed John would go far.

Due to his problem with numbers, everyone knew John was struggling in our statistics course. After the final exam, John, myself, the professor, and a couple of other classmates discussed some of the problems. Each question was multiple choice with five options. One by one we discussed the problems, and each time, John explained how he arrived at his answer. In every case, his explanation made no sense, indicating that he didn't understand the material at all. He got every question right. Here is an example. Solve for x.

$$x = 3^2$$

His thought process was something as nonsensical as this: "Well, three is squared, and squares have four sides ... You add it together and it's seven. Then you have to add the two above the three, so the answer is nine." Again, this happened three or four times in a row. I was astounded. Oh well, the universe is outcome oriented. John graduated with honors.

On paper, if you look at John and see that he graduated with honors with a master's degree in finance, you may assume that he is decent with numbers. You'd be wildly incorrect. To be fair, John is the exception to the rule, but he talks a good game, so watch out.

My focus on intelligence in this chapter isn't meant to make us more intelligent, though that may be a side effect. To defeat tribalism, we need to sincerely try to understand each other. You can only sincerely attempt to understand someone if you have an open mind. Having confidence that our current perspective is already optimal, or that our conversation partners aren't very bright, makes it nearly impossible to be open-minded. If your conversation partner is a fool, and you listen to her, what does that make you? We can't afford to let social interactions and generalizations about people bias us against coming together when a reasonable argument is presented.

To illustrate the importance of open-mindedness, we'll spectate the journey of a group of students in Mrs. Li's math class. Mrs. Li teaches at the hypothetical Iron Knee High School. All students in her class are required to complete a take-home math test. The highest-scoring students will have the option to join the Iron Knee High School math team.

The exam consists of a single problem with steps a–z. The outcome from each step is used as the input to the following step. It's graded by the rules of the universe; students only get credit for the number of right answers. They get no credit for performing the correct logic on bad inputs from prior steps. Since this is a take-home exam, students are permitted to research as much as they want in order to be successful.

It's common for political questions to be z-length problems like this math tryout. This is because political issues are built on top of concepts as intricate as worldviews. In a z-length problem, if you only make one mistake and it's on step y, it's not a huge deal. You'll be spot-on for most of the relevant concerns. If you only make one mistake and it's on step a … you're in trouble now. The universe is giving you no credit for b–z, and you got a wrong. Logically speaking, you got 25 out of 26 right. Factually speaking, you got 0 out of 26 right.

Let's give the person who made one mistake in part a a name; we'll call him Adam. Adam's answer for part a where he made a logical mistake was -1. The right answer for part a is 4. Part b asks you to take the square root of your answer from part a. For the majority of his classmates who got part a right, part b was a simple problem. Most of them knew that the square root of 4 is 2, and they moved on quickly. Adam, however, had quite the problem on his hands. What is the square root of -1? He tried a few numbers and quickly came to a frustrating conclusion. When positive numbers are squared, the result is positive, and when negative numbers are squared, the result is still positive. He couldn't fathom the square root of -1, because he wasn't aware of anything that could be squared to create a negative number.

Having exhausted his mental energy attempting to figure it out on its own, Adam decided to do some research. After a few Google searches, he comes across the concept of imaginary numbers, denoted by the variable, i. For those who aren't familiar with imaginary numbers, they are, I would say "real," but by definition they aren't "real" numbers. It is a real mathematical concept. Imaginary numbers blew Adam's mind. They seemed like a combination of math and philosophy. "Iron Knee High School must have a very advanced math team," he thought.

His curiosity pulled him forward. He read about the uses of imaginary numbers in advanced mathematics and quantum physics. He got exposed to new ideas he had never heard of before. He even practiced solving some advanced problems. Upon concluding his deep dive into college-level mathematics and physics, catalyzed by his exposure to imaginary numbers, he went back and finished the exam. The rest of the exam was easy compared to the difficult work he had just engaged in.

The next day at lunch before they turned in their exams, Adam was sitting at a table with Bob, Casey, and Diane. Adam asked how everyone felt about the difficulty of the assignment. Bob said it was very hard, so he was only able to complete the first three problems. This wasn't surprising. Everyone knew Bob didn't take school seriously, and he wasn't very bright on top of that.

Casey and Diane remarked that it was pretty easy. Adam knew they were better than average students, but he was surprised that no one brought up the incredibly difficult step b. Intrigued by their omission, Adam asked, "What answer did you guys get for step b?" All of them had the same answer: two. Passionately, Adam responds, "No, the answer isn't two. The answer is i, an imaginary number, they're really cool!"

Bob heartily laughed at Adam. "I thought Adam was supposed to be smart. He believes in imaginary numbers. I bet his answer in part c was the tooth fairy." Everyone joined in with Bob, laughing at Adam's supposed foolishness. Angry, and having lost faith in his classmates, Adam stormed off.

"Whatever ... these ignorant people don't even know what imaginary numbers are," Adam thought to himself. "They'll see when I have the best score and make the math team. After what I've learned, there is no way they are better than me at math."

After turning in their exams, they were promptly graded. By the end of the day, everyone's scores were posted on the board publicly. Casey had the top score in the class with 24/26 questions right. Diane had 19/26 right. Bob had 2/26 right. Adam had 0/26 right. Upon seeing the results, Adam was dumbfounded. There was no possible way he was the worst in the class. He knew he was the best.

Bob expected to score low since he only answered three questions, but upon seeing he beat Adam's score, he taunted him again. "It looks like you did put the tooth fairy for part c after all, didn't you!" This time it was in front of the entire class, not just the lunchroom table. Everyone laughed at Adam, and he had nowhere to go. He just sat silently, waited until the end of class, and then left.

Adam ended up hating everyone, and he obviously didn't make the math team. Since he didn't like them, he never ended up talking to them again. He knew with absolute certainty that no student in his entire school was better at math than he was. After he thought about it, he realized that Casey was the teacher's pet, and Bob had family in the school's administration. There was no way he scored worse than Bob. It had to have been a conspiracy against him.

After sulking for a few days, Adam went to the Internet to share the story of how he was cheated out of his position on the math team due to deep corruption within the school system. Before long, he found a social community of other students who were supposedly wronged in the same way. Some of these people knew more about imaginary numbers than even he did. He had found his community. Iron Knee High School's math team had a good season that year. Though they ended up losing the championship because no one knew how to do math involving imaginary numbers.

The end.

The universe is a cruel teacher. Unfortunately, I don't think we'll be getting a better substitute anytime soon. So how do we deal with this? With humility and good faith. One mistake everyone made in this story, is being overconfident due to something that they knew to be true. Adam knew he was better than everyone at math. This was true. This truth made him too arrogant to listen to his peers who didn't know what imaginary numbers were. The rest of his classmates knew Adam got literally every question wrong. This was true as well. This gave them confidence to dismiss what he had to say entirely and laugh at him.

The worst part of the story was that Adam and the rest of the class stopped talking. This was because they let their mathematical disagreements turn personal. Math differences grew into dislike, disrespect, and eventually hatred on Adam's part. If only his classmates were more willing to listen to him, they too would have learned about imaginary numbers. This would have increased their level of respect for Adam's skills in mathematics. Then they could have worked together to find out why Adam got 0/26 questions right.

With friends working alongside him, Adam wouldn't have had to jump to conclusions with conspiracy theories. Eventually they would have gotten to the root of the error, part *a*, and then life would have moved on peacefully for everyone. His classmates would have respect for Adam's skills, and Adam would be humbler moving forward, given his costly error. Everyone could have ended up smarter not by being smarter, but simply by having more humility and good faith. Iron Knee High School's math team certainly would have been better off with Adam in it.

Being Wrong Has Consequences

This story is interesting because it's real. Practically all of us have mistakes scattered across the mountain that makes up our current worldview. We don't know where the mistakes are, but they probably exist, and there are probably more than one. Internally, we need to make sure our fundamentals are correct. If the roots and the trunk are rotten, the rest of the tree doesn't matter very much.

When you encounter someone with an incredibly different worldview than you, arguing about step j may be as pointless as arguing in entirely different languages. Your d, e, f, g, h, i routes to j may not match. Both of you can have reasonable answers for j, given your answers for the preceding steps. The only chance you have of coming to an understanding, is to start with where you agree, and move forward until you get to the root of the divergence. In this example, it would mean starting at a, finding out you agree through c, and then noticing the disagreement begins at part d. You can have a productive conversation about d. If you succeed on d, the rest of the disagreements may resolve themselves.

A particularly frustrating thing for Adam, is how the rest of the class can't tell the difference between him and Bob. This happens in the real world too. It's difficult to judge how intelligent someone is based on beliefs alone. As we discussed, you're more likely to underestimate someone's intelligence if you disagree with them, and vice versa. If you go on outcomes alone, like the universe does, Bob is more correct than Adam. Yet Adam only made one logical error. If Bob had guessed and filled out the remaining questions, he very likely would have ended up making twenty-four logical errors.

Bob could have made twenty-four times the logical mistakes as Adam, and still scored better than him. Bob isn't as good at math as Adam is. Not even close. Regardless, due to the scores, he looks better, and Adam looks the complete fool. Every student who only made one logical error could be considered roughly equally good at math, but the scores could have ranged from 0/26 to 25/26. Those who made two logical errors could have scored from 0/26 to 24/26. The only difference is whether they were wrong earlier or later in the chain.

Progress and improvement build confidence, unfortunately. I often see a sort of "education" system arise in groups of people like Adam who are all practically entirely wrong. Adam is perceived as a wise man in his community. Adam's only mistake was in part a. This community bonds together because they all got part a wrong. However, many of them have also made other logical mistakes, for example on parts j, o, and z.

Wise math guru Adam will educate them on the errors of their ways for those three steps. Each time they are corrected by Adam, the entire picture makes more sense to them. They are becoming optimally wrong together. Learning like this isn't necessarily bad. The problem is that this real process of improvement often makes them less likely to listen to people who didn't get part a wrong.

So, who are you? Adam? Diane? Hopefully not Bob. I don't know, and you can't either. Worry not; if you choose to practice humility and good faith, you'll become smarter than all of them anyway.

Not Wrong, Just Wrong

Very few of us are Bob. Thinking that Bob makes up the majority of the opposite political party is a mistake. This simply is not true, and I'm happy it's not true. There are, however, a lot of people who are rational 80% of the time, but are wrong in a few key places. Though there may only be a few sources of their errors, each error causes a chain reaction of consequences. So many consequences that they end up blending in with Bob.

Here is a good litmus test to separate Bobs from regular people who are wrong in consequential places. Ask yourself the following question. If I believed the fundamentals of what they believe, would their behavior and other beliefs make sense? Usually they do make sense, and you're not dealing with Bob. If their belief system is in conflict with itself, even if you assume the fundamentals are true, you may be dealing with Bob. No offense to anyone named Bob, though I doubt Bob would be reading this book.

I was watching a video of an angry MAGA mob somewhere, and a member of the crowd, we'll call him Terry, asked the following question. "How many elections are we going to let them steal before we use our guns?"

My first thought was, "This is dangerous, our politics are getting out of hand." My second thought was, "That's actually a reasonable question if you believe the election was stolen."

Are you just going to let the tyrannical villains win every time and accept it forever? For those of you who think violence is never the answer, what do you call the American Revolution? "No taxation without representation" led to war. If representation isn't relevant because elections are being stolen, it's a similar situation. I can't say that Terry is wrong. He's just wrong.

How can Terry be both wrong and not wrong at the same time? Allow me to explain. There are two types of disagreements people can have. Fundamental disagreements and factual disagreements. The only disagreements worth judging someone negatively for are fundamental disagreements.

Fundamentally, I agree with Terry that we can't allow corrupt politicians to steal elections. In this regard, he is not wrong. Factually, we disagree about whether or not the 2020 election was stolen. He thinks the deep state robbed Trump of his rightful victory. I think Trump tried to do the very thing he's criticizing the deep state of doing. We disagree factually, but fundamentally we're nearly the same.

People don't often think about why they disagree with someone. About whether the disagreement is factual or fundamental. After all, if you're a tribal thinker, regardless of the reason, you're still on opposite sides. If instead you're a principled thinker, you'll recognize and appreciate the blessing of a purely factual disagreement. This means that you and the person with whom you have the disagreement are fundamentally the same. The path to resolving the dispute is clear. Iron out the facts, then you will be in agreement. Agreeing on the facts, but disagreeing on the fundamentals is much harder to resolve.

In a discussion about the consequences of being wrong, it would be criminal to omit this quote from writer and philosopher Voltaire.

"Those who can make you believe absurdities can make you commit atrocities."

Imagine we polled one hundred people with questions about when violence is justified. One of the questions was the following. "Would you feel justified using lethal force to defend against a genocide of your people?" How many would say yes? I don't know, but I would say yes, and I doubt I'd be alone.

Now consider this fact. Some far-right extremists believe that Jewish people are trying to commit genocide against the White race. This creates a factual disagreement that is pretty important, doesn't it? On May 14, 2022, eighteen-year-old domestic terrorist Payton Gendron brutally killed ten innocent people at a supermarket in a Black community. He was motivated to take action because he believed in this supposed genocide of the White race.

Was Gendron wrong fundamentally? Not if you said you'd use lethal force to defend against a genocide of your people. That means we have a factual disagreement. I don't claim to understand how murdering innocent Black people protects White people from Jewish people, but that's a separate conversation. Many news sources described him as "pure evil." Based on his actions, that's an entirely understandable takeaway. It feels *right* to call him evil. Though if we actually want to solve the problem, *evil* is not accurate enough.

Among other things, Mr. Gendron was one of my inspirations for writing this book. Before he committed the terroristic atrocity, he wrote a 180-page manifesto outlining the justifications for his fears, hatred, and murderous intent. He believed he was right; he didn't think he was evil. He probably thought of himself as a martyr. I figured, if he can write 180 pages of hateful garbage encouraging us to kill each other, the least I could do is try to put something out there in the opposite direction.

Religious disagreements are factual disagreements as well. Though factual disagreements are usually the easiest to resolve, religion is the exception. Factual disagreements about religious claims are practically impossible to settle.

Most of the time, religious disagreements don't impact the earthly world, so they don't matter. If one person believes someone lived in the stomach of a whale, and another believes that the whale was their reincarnated grandmother, both may think the other is a fool, but the consequences end there. However, when a factual religious disagreement is the cause of violent conflict, the conflict can become perpetual. Sunni and Shia Muslims have been in conflict for over one thousand years, and they're both Muslims.

Due to our short historical attention spans, religious violence and extremism are often portrayed as issues specific to Islam. The fact is, Islam is far from the only religion with a history of violence. There were the Crusades by Christians in the twelfth and thirteenth centuries, and the Inquisition by Catholics in the sixteenth century. As we discussed before, there are plenty of other religions besides the few we often think about. Many of those have been sources of violent conflict throughout history as well.

One common defense of religious violence is to claim that it's only an issue due to "extremists." I actually agree with this point to some extent. Unfortunately, I think there will always be extremists. I'm all for doing what we can to reduce religious extremism, but I'm not confident in how effective we can be.

Here is why I believe religious extremists are practically inevitable. In extreme situations, extreme behavior becomes reasonable behavior. Religion puts us in extreme situations. To showcase what I mean, let's start with a popular ethical dilemma thought experiment called the trolley problem.

There are five innocent people tied to train tracks. The train you're on will soon run them over, killing them all. You're unable to stop the train. The good news is, you can switch onto an alternative track. The bad news is, there is one innocent person tied to the other track. Do you switch tracks? If you do, you cause someone who would have otherwise lived to die, but save five lives in the process. If you don't switch tracks, you let five people die to avoid killing the single person on the other track.

I've seen research claiming that somewhere north of 80% of people would change tracks to kill one innocent person instead of five. I imagine most of the remaining 20% would eventually swap tracks as the numbers on the main track grew from five, to fifty, to five hundred, to five thousand, and so on. I also imagine there are a few people who would run over the entire world before they changed the tracks because they don't want "blood on their hands" for the murder of the one person. I understand them I guess, but I don't want them making decisions in these kinds of situations.

This is about to be uncomfortable. We prefer to think about extremist religious terrorists as "pure evil," but let's try to sincerely understand them as they truly are. As we increase the number of people on the main track, we become more confident in our decision to switch tracks, right? The vast majority of people will. Notice that we've been talking about finite numbers here. Religion introduces the concept of the afterlife. Ideas like heaven and hell, for example. I can't fathom a more extreme difference than the difference between heaven and hell. Heaven is basically infinitely good, and hell is infinitely bad.

What would you be willing to do to avoid an infinite bad? Logically speaking, anything finitely bad would be justifiable. If hell were introduced to the trolley problem on the current track, it would be reasonable to do practically anything to swap the tracks. What if on the alternate side of the track was the murder of all humans on the planet, causing our extinction? That's horrible, right? Yes, it's horrible at the scale of the murder of eight billion people. That's minuscule, infinitesimal compared to one infinite amount of horribleness represented by hell. It's not even close. All finite additions pale in comparison to any infinite.

Envision a religious extremist named Benjamin, who believes that his God wants him to execute a second terror attack on the scale of 9/11. Benjamin is honored to be part of his God's plan. He doesn't see this as an act of terrorism. He sees it as the greatest privilege. To sacrifice his life for the mission of his Heavenly Father.

He believes that the end result of his actions will be more people in heaven, including himself, and fewer innocent people in hell. Before he commits the atrocity, he has one last meal with his family. He hugs his mother, gives gifts to his nieces and nephews, and then departs to do "God's work."

We see the results of Benjamin's atrocity, but we don't see the buildup. We can't really criticize him fundamentally. Who would have the audacity to defy God himself? Especially if you believe God is infinitely smarter and more moral than you are. We can disagree factually, and claim that his God doesn't exist, or that his God doesn't want him to be a terrorist. Good luck convincing anyone that their understanding of religion is wrong. At the end of the day, Benjamin is doing the trolley problem just like we were. It's just that the stakes are infinitely extreme due to his religion bringing in the concepts of heaven and hell. Fundamentally, he could just be trying to maximize positivity in the afterlife.

What happens when Benjamin gets hold of a nuclear weapon? Nuclear weapons are horrible. More horrible than *The Hostile Hospital*. So horrible they come with a silver lining, mutually assured destruction. That means if we fight a nuclear war, we all lose.

You may not know this, but you woke up this morning because Vladimir Putin allowed you to wake up. If he wanted to conduct a preemptive first strike against us with Russia's nuclear arsenal, we're done for. Game over. However, Putin knows that if he does this, Russia is going down with us, and he doesn't want to die either. This is about as stable of a situation as we can get with the existence of these world-changing weapons.

Someone threatens to kill you, you threaten to kill them, and then we have peace. The best we flawed humans can do. Benjamin promises to kill you, and he is ready to die himself because heaven awaits. What can you say to Benjamin? I have no idea. You better convince him out of his religious beliefs very quickly, which almost certainly won't work. Then it's over.

In the previous chapter on societal contexts, I urged religious tolerance. I did so because it is possible, though not certain, that religion provides a net positive effect on societies. However, nuclear weapons exist, and even greater military technology will in the future. If we want to survive another one thousand years, I believe we'll need to figure out a way to achieve stable, lasting peace. As I'm writing this, the Doomsday Clock managed by the Bulletin of the Atomic Scientists is at ninety seconds from midnight. The ability to make peace with each other may well be the test of humanity as a species. I don't think we can attain the peace we need to survive in the long run if we're still fighting each other over unresolvable religious differences.

The fragility of the human experiment moving forward is mostly due to our increasing military strength, not religious differences. I just see religious conflict as another barrier to peace. A unique one, given that it can't be solved factually, so I don't know what we can do about it.

To those who think I'm overreacting about nuclear risk, remember that nuclear weapons are technology of the microwave oven era. We've done pretty well with carrots and sticks to prevent more countries from getting them. Still, over time, more countries will have them. I don't want more Vladimir Putins, Kim Jong Uns, or Osama Bin Ladens deciding whether or not I'll wake up in the morning.

Before the nuclear weapon, we didn't have the means to fail as a species. No matter what we did, we couldn't kill enough of each other to threaten *Homo sapiens*. Now we can. Humans have been around for quite a while and we haven't failed yet. However, we just took the training wheels off, so don't be overconfident.

8. Inclusion 2.0

"Do I not destroy my enemies when I make them my friends?"
— Abraham Lincoln

♫ Blues on the Banjo | Fruteland Jackson

Are White people a minority? It depends on the context. In the United States, they're about 60% of the population. In the context of the nation as a whole, no, White people are not a minority. In the context of the neighborhoods I grew up in, they were a minority.

I like to think I know a bit about those White people's experiences. Though I'm not White, I'm very light-skinned; so light, that in a room full of Black kids I was, comparatively, the "White" one. What do you think the stereotypes are for White boys surrounded by Black boys in a low-income inner-city school district? Smart, well-behaved, weak. I was smart and well-behaved. I got tested on the weak part.

I think my father predicted this would happen due to my skin color and demeanor. To bullies looking for someone to pick on at low-risk, I looked a fine target. In preparation, he taught me how to fight in advance of even elementary school. I was no MMA fighter, but I could throw a punch with good form and put my body weight into it. Plus, after sparring with my dad, I didn't have much fear of a fair fight with kids my own size. I had to defend myself physically from time to time. Most often from new kids who didn't know my history.

I'd rather not have had to defend myself in that way, but at least I was prepared. Many of my White classmates weren't prepared. They were afraid of conflict. That meant the bully didn't just fight them once like in my case. They were bothered daily. Early in elementary school, I used to fight bullies for those who were too afraid to defend themselves. Eventually I got into too much trouble personally, and had to stop.

Not all, but some of those White kids had hard lives being a minority in Black majority areas. Do you think they care that people with their skin tone have more wealth on average than people with darker skin tones while their faces are being pushed into the dirt? They went to school with us, so many of them were as poor as everyone else. I imagine them today, interacting with liberals telling them how privileged they are. In that conversation, I wouldn't blame them for siding with conservatives.

To be successful as a party, we need to win the working class. That includes White people. Liberals are hopeful that demographic shifts will be wind in our sails in the long run. As the country becomes more diverse, we expect that it will be easier for us to win. This may be true to some extent, though I suspect not as much as we hope. If demographic change is a boon in the long run, that's great, but the last thing we want to do is make an enemy out of White people.

Don't Make Unnecessary Enemies

What does a White man get for voting Democrat besides the ability to virtue signal in mainstream society? I could name plenty of reasons it would be in the average White man's interest to vote Democrat. The fact that I can answer the question doesn't matter. How many reasons could you come up with? Take your time and think about it. If you're a liberal, whatever you thought of doesn't matter either.

How many reasons could a conservative or an independent come up with? That's the question that matters. I don't think they would be able to find many reasons, and that's a failure on our part. Supporting women, minorities, and other historically oppressed groups is great. We should continue to do that, but without helping conservatives paint the picture that we're against White men.

People are self-interested. Every time a conservative pundit criticizes "woke" diversity and inclusion programs, there is a subtle "we're on your side" message to White people. Simply by rejecting diversity as an intrinsic good, they seem pro-White. This supposed trade-off between helping minorities and helping White people makes intuitive sense, but it doesn't have to be a zero-sum game.

Minorities don't have to benefit at the expense of the majority. We can try to reduce police brutality in Black communities with things like better oversight and bodycams, while still trying to make White people feel welcome at the table. I've seen people on the far left scream, "You're a White male!" to simply disqualify a White man's opinion due to his identity. I don't think that was part of Dr. King's dream.

I remember when I first heard from a fellow liberal that we Black people can't be racist. I was eating lunch in the cafeteria my sophomore year in college at an HBCU. The classmate saying this was a Black woman and, from what I heard, she was a good student. Upon hearing her opening statement, I responded, "Of course Black people can be racist. Old Black people are some of the most racist people I know. It's likely because old Black people had the worst racial experiences, so they have better reasons."

She responded, "They may not like White people, but racism is prejudice plus power, and Black people don't have the institutional power to be racist."

"Just because you don't have power doesn't mean you're not racist," I replied.

"Yes, it does," she said matter-of-factly.

There was nowhere to go from there; we simply defined racism differently. I can understand prejudice plus power being the recipe needed to implement long-lasting institutional racism. However, deciding that power is a necessity for racism simply changes the core meaning of the word. It doesn't matter what words mean really. If the words *racism* and *autism* changed meanings, the world would keep turning. Though if people haven't caught on yet, you can't blame them for judging you when you say your child isn't racist, but he's on the spectrum. Likewise, her holier-than-thou Black exemption from autism, I mean racism, isn't going to help us win votes in rural White areas.

I'm not saying we need a platform of policies to address White-only issues. I don't lose any sleep over "reverse racism." However, even though we may not take reverse racism very seriously, one of the easiest ways to enrage someone is to tell them how they feel isn't real. What they feel is a factual truth of the universe. They may be feeling it based on faulty information, or out of bias. Yet they do, truthfully, feel it.

Even writing this, I'm tempted to make fun of White men feeling sorry for themselves about reverse racism. To make a joke about who the real snowflakes are, but I won't go there. Though it may score points among ourselves, we'd just be pushing them further away from us. As we're laughing, we're losing.

The social environment we create on the left appears to make White identity a bad thing. Even if you don't feel that way as a liberal, it seems that way to many independents and conservatives. We celebrate when women and minorities achieve great things. The vast majority of us do this because of the long history of real discrimination; we're happy to see evidence of a fairer playing field. There is no malice or anti-White sentiment in this perspective, but it feels bad as a White person to know you'd be more appreciated in this community if you were a minority.

Though the vast majority of us don't have an anti-White disposition as we celebrate the achievements of other groups, some of us do. Dr. King's central message wasn't pro-Black, it was antidiscrimination. It was effectively pro-Black, which is why it's easy to get confused. Over time, pro-Black sentiment can transform into anti-White sentiment. Though this only happens to a minority of liberals, it happens to enough of us to provide a steady stream of content to conservative fearmongers. If mainstream liberals are too timid to rebuff anti-White elements within our party, it will be to our party's detriment, as well as the country's.

Our core message shouldn't be a divisive topic like diversity, equity, and inclusion. It's bad marketing, but it's also bad governance, which contributes to the problem of tribalism. We shouldn't play politics by winning, and then catering to the special interest groups who supported us. Our job is to make the country a better place for all Americans, not just the 51% who voted for us. It shouldn't feel like White people win when conservatives are elected, and minorities win when liberals are elected. It shouldn't feel that way, but to many people it does, and it's our fault for emphasizing identity too much.

In our marketing and governance platforms, we should prioritize policies that are good for the vast majority of Americans. Things like our unwavering commitment to Social Security, in contrast with some Republicans who want to cut the program. Our commitment to improving public education. Our willingness to use safety regulations to protect communities from events like the train derailment in East Palestine, Ohio, in 2023. I could go on, but you get the point. Emphasize our policies that are better for the vast majority of Americans, including White people. It's good governance, it's honorable, it creates a bigger tent, and reduces tribalism.

Another group of people we make unnecessary enemies out of are the wealthy. The wealthy only make up the top few percent by definition. They can't influence elections much by voting; they influence elections monetarily. However, even their money only goes so far. How many pro-Democrat ads would you have to pay for to weaken Donald Trump's grip on the MAGA base? You could pay for all of them and barely diminish his support.

If money bought elections, Obama and Trump, despite how rich Trump wants you to think he is, couldn't have won. Of course, the political machines behind each party will have a lot of money available for whoever becomes the party's nominee. Before that point, however, wealthy people can't just pick the leader they want. Ask Michael Bloomberg. Wealthy people have a variety of political views as well; it's not like they are a homogenous group with a single agenda. Wealthy individuals can try to influence us with ads, but at the end of the day, the top 1% only has 1% of the votes. We have the rest.

As humans, we need to mature past always needing an enemy to rally against. Populists on the left and the right agree that we need to focus on the wealthy as the true enemy. Even some people I respect like Dr. Cornel West have a strong anti-wealthy agenda. Dr. West is running for president in 2024. He recently showed up on Fox News to be interviewed by conservative political pundit Laura Ingraham. He criticized Governor Ron DeSantis for having a "xenophobic dimension" with his flavor of populism. He was criticizing DeSantis for supposedly trying to play poor Whites against poor immigrants.

Dr. West's implied wiser position was to encourage "the workers of all colors to come together against the bosses." Simply put, Dr. West thinks it's unwise to play Whites against Hispanics, but it's wise to play the poor against the rich. It seems to me Dr. West still has an extra step to take in his journey to wisdom on this topic. Dr. West's message is that different colors of poor people forming groups and pointing fingers at each other needs to stop. Instead, they need to point fingers at the wealthy group of people. My message is to stop feeling the need to point fingers at entire groups of people, period.

Dr. West is a successful man himself; should we be pointing at him? Oh, but he is one of the good ones, is he? Then there must be other good ones besides him, right? If so, I'd feel mightily stupid for pointing the finger at them just because some other rich people are bad. How about we just put our fingers down and come together? Why do we always have to be against some other group?

Musician Oliver Anthony struck a chord with the anti-wealthy movements on both sides of the aisle in his hit song "Rich Men North of Richmond." Personally, I like the song. Music is art. Like comedy, it doesn't have to be philosophically perfect. Since this is the case, I'm not criticizing him for his song. It's beautiful as is. However, if I were to examine it seriously and philosophically, I would criticize the need to generalize wealthy people as the source of our problems.

Most of us have learned not to generalize on the basis of race. We haven't learned the fundamental lesson, however, because the same behavior on the basis of wealth evades our moral alarms. "Mexicans South of Lexington" sounds wrong. "Rich Men North of Richmond" sounds right. Generalize and blame based on race. Generalize and blame based on wealth. What's the difference? No one feels bad for rich people? I understand feeling that way, but wrong is wrong.

I'm not rich myself, but I know a handful of wealthy people. To varying degrees, I've interacted with highly esteemed professors, a Grammy Award-winning musician, and executives in investment management companies. These are all top 1%–3% types of people. I don't personally know a statistically significant sample of very high net worth individuals. Anecdotally, from a moral perspective, they don't seem much different than the average person. They can even seem more generous at times, due to the simple fact that they don't need money anymore. They still want more money of course, but not needing it changes your relationship to it.

Most of them didn't start off wealthy. They also avoided becoming noticeably mean or greedy after they became millionaires. One of the executives at a mutual fund company I interned with in Chicago started an organization to help the needy in Tanzania. I don't recall the details, but he had an organization there that helped the locals. If you simply saw him as a suit who gets rich with financial wizardry moving money around, you'd be oversimplifying at the very least. Would you do as much for Africans as he did if you had his money? I don't know, but you'd be wrong to judge him simply because of his profession, wealth, or skin color.

The highly successful people I know tend to be experts who are passionate about what they do, and managed to stick with it for many years. Simply put, most of them were otherwise regular people with some combination of expertise and persistence. They are people that many of us could learn something from, and certainly have no business pointing fingers at.

I support raising taxes on the wealthy, and not just income taxes. I'm talking about where they really make their money, capital gains taxes. The policies alone get the job done. We can make it harder to be highly wealthy without making enemies out of them.

Though I support more progressive taxes, I don't believe that increasing taxes on the rich will directly help poor people. Poor people need a lot of help. Even if we took all of the wealth from the top 1% and redistributed it evenly across the bottom 10%, we'd still have a long-term poverty problem to address. It's easy to point fingers at the rich, but it isn't effective. Improving the lives of the poor in the long run isn't as simple as wealth redistribution. It would require a multifaceted approach aimed at moving closer to equal opportunity, and making cultural improvements. This is difficult work.

Wealthy people being wealthy isn't a problem. If you somehow became rich tomorrow, I'd be happy for you; it doesn't hurt me if you're rich. Wealth isn't bad, poverty is bad. Instead of being against the wealthy, let's be against the situation where working people are still in poverty. I encourage you to practice replacing something more abstract with any group of people you don't like.

Instead of being against White men, be against racism. Instead of being against Black people, be against whatever you don't like about Black people, like urban fashion or high crime rates. Instead of being against Jews, be against whatever you don't like about Jews, like corruption. Instead of being against Russians, be against bigger countries taking land from smaller countries by force. When you generalize a group of people as an enemy, you're almost always going to be wrong. Most of us know this by now when it comes to race. Let's stop making the same mistake when the groups are defined by something other than skin color.

Don't Be a Zealot

Have you ever visited someone, and their home seemed perfect? I'm not talking about an expensive home, but a place where everything is extremely clean and organized. A place where you're asked to take off your shoes, and everyone is perfectly respectful, polite, and politically correct. It's uncomfortable, isn't it? That's how the Democratic Party feels to many outside the party, and some within it.

We have to get out of the business of enforcing goodness. People don't have to be good. They have to not be bad. By "bad," I mean committing criminal acts. You want to be the optimal human? Great, that's an honorable endeavor, but it's perfectly fine to simply not be a criminal. Speaking of criminals, talking to Democrats can feel like talking to the police; no one wants to talk to the police.

When the police stop bad things from happening like domestic violence, or bank robberies, they are hailed as heroes. How would you feel if the police started enforcing goodness? It's seven o'clock on a Saturday morning, and the police start banging on your door. Groggy, you throw on something presentable before greeting them. When you open the door, Officer Jared asks you to explain why you didn't wake up early and get a head start on the day. Sure, the optimally productive version of yourself may wake up early on Saturdays to do something positive for the community or your family. Though it would be nice, that's not Officer Jared's business, is it?

Later that morning, Quincy was driving to work and got pulled over by a cop. Quincy didn't know what he did wrong, so he said, "Good morning, Officer, what's going on?"

Officer Jared began writing a citation while replying, "Are you aware that you were going thirty-seven miles per hour in a thirty-five-mile-per-hour zone?"

Quincy was furious. "Just my luck," he thought to himself. "I'm sorry, Officer, but is it even legal to pull someone over for going two miles per hour over the speed limit? This has never happened to me before, and it seems like you're trying to bother me specifically."

Indignant, Jared answered, "Woah now, I don't like your tone. Accusing me of trying to bother you as if I'm corrupt? Those words feel like violence to me, I'm going to have to take you to jail for assaulting an officer. You won't be able to see a judge until Monday, so you'll be there for the weekend. Please turn around and put your hands behind your back while I read you your rights."

"This is a joke, right?" scoffed Quincy.

"Shall I add resisting arrest to your charges?" quipped Officer Jared.

"No, sir."

Jared proceeds to handcuff Quincy and read him his Miranda rights. While Quincy was cuffed in the back seat of the police car on the way to jail, Jared tells him, "You know, Quincy, I'm running for county sheriff. Now that we've gotten to know each other, I would appreciate it if you voted for me."

This may seem like an extreme story, but people who aren't on the left often feel like Quincy. They worry that if they accidentally misgender a trans person it will make them seem transphobic.

Being known as a transphobe could cause them to lose their livelihood and, consequently, their ability to provide for their family. Regardless of how likely it is to happen, it's a fact that people feel that way. Those feelings have consequences, one of which, is that they aren't going to vote for us.

Another bad habit we need to drop is defining how fair something is based on equality of outcome. The fundamental left-wing argument goes something like this: No group of people is superior to another. That means everything should be proportional. If the world were fair, 50% of CEOs would be female, each ethnicity would be reflected in Congress proportional to its share of the general population, and so on. I understand the argument, and the people who believe this have their hearts in the right place. However, I'd like to ask a question. Why are there women's chess tournaments?

I remember watching a women's chess tournament and asking myself, "Why am I watching a women's chess tournament?" Not because the chess was bad; the women were all far better than me. I wanted to know why they divided chess by gender.

I can understand men not competing with women in weightlifting or sprinting. If they did, women simply wouldn't be competitive, and it would effectively just be men's weightlifting and sprinting. To allow women to even compete, they need their own leagues for those two sports. However, that argument didn't make sense to me for chess.

It's not like chess is incredibly demanding physically. I don't believe men are born with a "chess gene" women don't have. I don't think men are more intelligent or strategic than women. So why do we need a separate league for women's chess? Essentially, for the same reason we need a separate league for women's track and field.

Because without a women's league, it would just be men's chess, with a few exceptions like Grandmaster Judit Polgár.

It doesn't make much sense to jump to "discrimination" as an explanation. The best women simply lose to the best men at higher rates than they win. "Discrimination" isn't going to move chess pieces for you or your opponent. If it's not discrimination, and it's not a genetic disadvantage, why are the best women worse than the best men at chess?

I don't know, but I suspect more young boys commit a large portion of their lives to chess than young girls do. Suppose that there are fifteen boys for every one girl who commits their life to chess, and in the top chess rankings nine out of ten players are male. This would indicate that women are better than men at chess; they would be overrepresented based on those who actually tried. Based on the sheer quantity of boys dedicating their lives to chess, it looks like we're better than women, though we may actually be worse. I don't know if this is true, but it seems plausible to me.

If it is true that boys commit to chess from a young age at a rate multiple times higher than the rate for girls, how does it make sense to expect 50% female representation in top chess players? The only way to get 50% female chess players at the top would be to prevent boys from playing or, perhaps, to force more girls to play. That doesn't seem reasonable, does it?

Let's switch to a corporate context. How many men dedicate their lives to climbing the corporate ladder compared to women? If men and women aren't trying equally hard, I wouldn't expect equal results. I'm a man, and I don't care much about the corporate ladder, so I'm certainly not judging women who think like I do. If we find specific evidence of glass ceilings and sexism, it's already against the law; we should enforce it, and take the criminals down.

However, the lack of proportional representation in an institution doesn't indicate foul play.

The Lesser of Two Evils

Let's put ourselves in the minds of two independents considering which party to vote for in the next election. We'll call these independents Jack and Jill. Republicans and Democrats have stands they can visit to learn more about their party. First, Jack decides to approach the Democrat stand while Jill watches.

Jack walks over and says, "Hey, guys, how's it going?" Immediately all the Democrats gasp in horror at the atrocity that just occurred. Did he just say "guys" to a group that included women? Did he ignore the fact that women might be uncomfortable with that? Is he assuming our genders? Does he even know that gender is a social construct?

Based on the disgust on their faces, he knows he just lost respect from all the Democrats in the area. One of them asks him if he is a sexist, and he regrets having even walked over. He leaves the Democratic stand before a conversation even gets started. We lost Jack for sure. More importantly, we lost Jill, and any other independents who just saw that interaction.

Next, Jill decides to visit the Republican stand. The people weren't nearly as judgmental of her. However, after speaking with them, she realized how deep the conspiracies are, and the fact that their glorious leader only believes in democracy when it rules in his favor. The more the results show him winning, the more correct they must be, and vice versa. Jill returns to Jack, and they have no idea what to do. The only reason it's even close is because of how bad the Republican Party is. Discouraged by their options, they decide to pick what they believe to be the lesser of two evils on election day.

With social media, and the conservative desire to make liberals look as bad as possible, we see this story all the time. The sad part is, Jack felt like he didn't belong in the Democratic Party before we even had a chance to discuss any policies. At least Jill first felt welcome, and then was turned off by Republican policies. Jack just failed the virtue purity test, and felt like he didn't belong in the club. We can't afford to lose voters before we even talk policy.

Many people don't feel "good enough" to be liberals. They don't know the "prejudice plus power" equation. They don't care if people's feelings are hurt. They aren't interested in learning how the United States started in 1619 instead of 1776. They don't want to have to discuss trans issues with their children. Does this mean they are bad people? Of course not. Some liberals are purists who would be of the opinion that we don't want these people's votes. From the liberal purist's perspective, they aren't "woke" enough to be worthy members of our party. The end result of this "purity" is that we're going to be purely without power, having handed the reins over to the far right.

The modern Republican Party is very bad. Even many Republicans don't like the Republican Party. It's way worse than it used to be, and I couldn't have imagined myself saying that twenty years ago. Yet still, we're not the clear choice between the "lesser of two evils" for independents like Jack and Jill. We should be ashamed of ourselves for not being able to wipe the floor with the modern Republican Party, as weak as it is.

I remember when Donald Trump officially won the Republican nomination for president in 2016. I was speaking with my father and I said, "It's high risk, high reward." He asked what I meant, and I replied, "The high reward is that Trump should be the easiest Republican for Hillary to beat. The high risk is that if she doesn't beat him, we're in trouble."

Donald Trump is an honest liar. When he lies to you, it feels good. Off the cuff. From the hip. With a joking smile on his face. It's not right, but it feels right. Hillary Clinton, even when she's telling you the truth, it feels like she's lying to you. The truth matters, but how people feel matters too. If you want to win, anyway.

Many people, especially conservatives, will believe I was exaggerating about the risk Trump posed. After all, there was no catastrophe during Trump's presidency, and the economy was pretty good overall, right? At a surface level this is true. However, I don't like engaging in the myopic wishful thinking and excuse-making both parties do as it relates to the quality of their president. When your president is in office, anything good that happens is because of your president, and anything bad that happens was inherited from the previous administration.

Sometimes bad things happen that aren't the president's fault, like 9/11. Gas prices could go down due to global macroeconomic forces larger than the United States, and then fools are going to talk about how good their president is. You might as well thank the president for a sunny day, or blame him for the birds that painted your windshield.

The country didn't explode with Trump. It wasn't an absolute catastrophe, but the very foundation of our nation has been weakened. Our ability to trust our intuitions, our elections, each other. The common fabric that brought us together as a country is deteriorating. It wasn't all Trump's fault; it began before Trump stepped into the political arena. Darkness, hatred, and pessimism have been within us the entire time.

Trump created a context where our worst inclinations, on both sides, would be brought to the forefront. The cost was the social, political, and institutional unraveling of our country. Our house remains standing, but the foundation is crumbling. You can still look out the window and see a sunny day. Things feel close enough to "normal" for now, but we have serious work to do to shore up our infrastructure.

How did Trump create a context that was near-optimal for the unchecked growth of tribalism? He embraced his role as the anti-deep-state hero who would challenge the establishment and "save the children." He convinced his staunch supporters and many other Republicans to lose faith in elections. To the MAGA crowd, Trump couldn't have lost; the election had to have been stolen by the elites. Who are the powerful elites he is fighting against? This question leads his supporters into far-right antisemitic Jewish conspiracy theories. This results in violence against Jews, but also a belief in the "Great Replacement theory," which motivates domestic terrorists to kill minorities as well. Cue Payton Gendron.

Trump embraces the few true racists left in America, and antisemites about as much as possible while still retaining plausible deniability and electability. If I were a leader of one of those extreme domestic groups, I'd accept that Trump is the best we can possibly get for our agenda, and still have a chance of winning a national election.

Not only did Trump embrace almost everyone who supported him, no matter how questionable, he worked to get more right-wing extremists in office. Not because of policy, but because they would be the most loyal to him, which is what matters from his perspective. We have a strong system of checks and balances that is designed to handle a few bad apples. It's not designed to handle bushels of bad apples. We made it past January 6 because enough Republicans still had honor. However, those honorable Republicans, or as the far right would call them, RINOs, had targets on their backs for not being loyal to Trump. Many of them are already out of government.

The Republican Party is in bad shape. As liberals, we shouldn't celebrate this; it's bad for the country. Even if we can't get to "good," we should at least obviously be the lesser of two evils for anyone outside the MAGA crowd. Unfortunately, it's not obvious at all.

Populists for the Wealthy

Politics in the United States boils down to a choice between two parties. Occasionally there will be third-party distractions that damage whichever party they are closest to. Overall, however, we as Democrats only need to worry about Republicans. You can see their strategy for attacking us in real time by simply watching them. Most of it is fearmongering around the culture wars.

Conservatives know they need to win the working class too. They attempt to portray themselves as America-first patriots, supporting working families across the nation. They sell this narrative with their talking points, but their policies contradict them. Conservatives are overwhelmingly for deregulating companies and cutting taxes for corporations and the wealthy. Donald Trump cut the corporate tax rate from 35% to 21%. If I'm an owner of a large company, I'm delighted by this change. Sure, it will lower the government's tax revenue by tens of billions per year, but at least rich people who own companies get richer, right? For those unfamiliar with how large companies are valued, let's take a quick detour. We'll come back later to how conservatives try to paint themselves as populists while pursuing policies that help the rich get richer.

How much is $1 million per year forever worth? Well, $1 million per year for two years intuitively should be worth around $2 million, right? Forever is infinite years into the future, so does that mean $1 million forever is worth infinite money? If so, then how much would $2 million forever be worth? Two infinite monies? Forever is a long time; the fact that you'll get $1 million one thousand years from now isn't very useful, is it?

How much money would you be willing to accept today in exchange for the right to get $1 million in one thousand years? It probably wouldn't be much. Maybe $50 or something, since you'll likely be long dead before you get the $1 million anyway. What this means is $1 million forever from now is worth $0, $1 million one thousand years from now is worth very little, $1 million a year from now is worth something close to $1 million, and $1 million today is worth $1 million. In finance, we call this phenomenon the *time value of money*.

The time value of money is relevant because corporations make money every year. Companies don't have an expiration date. In theory, they can live forever. Imagine Apple is simply a machine that prints x billion dollars per year forever. To find the value of Apple, we need to add up the "present" value of all the future money Apple will make. This means the money it makes this year x, plus the money we think it will make next year, but discounted because money next year isn't as valuable as money this year based on the time value of money. You add these billions together with bigger discounts the further into the future you go, and you end up with the *net present value*. This represents the present value of all the money Apple will make forever.

Most of a company's value resides in the money we expect it to make in the future, not what it has today, or will make this year. This means that if Apple makes x billion dollars per year, Apple is going to be worth multiple times x, because of all the future money we think Apple will make going forward. For example, Apple made about $100 billion in free cash flow in 2022. The value of all of Apple's shares at the time of writing is around $2.8 trillion. The entire value of $2.8 trillion can be broken down into two categories. One is the value of the assets it currently has. The other is the future expectations of the money Apple will make, which is much bigger.

If we define x as the cash a company will generate every year, taxes lower the value of x. Intuitively, people think that the benefit of Trump's corporate tax cuts is that companies will save some money on their tax bills next year. That will happen too, but more importantly for an owner of the company, all of those future x values that get added up to determine the value of the company *all* just got bigger, instantly.

This is a simplified picture to avoid an entire chapter on finance principles, formulas, and mathematics. The point is to explain how tax rates don't just impact the company's tax bills this year; they impact the present value of the company itself based on the projected larger cash flows it will receive in future years. Since most of a company's value is based on money it is projected to make in the future, this is a much bigger deal than it appears to be.

As you can see, conservative policies work wonders for the rich. While I was studying business in graduate school, the vast majority of students were conservatives. The majority of professors were liberals, at least the ones comfortable sharing their broad political views. The professors don't usually run companies, but the students will.

Approximately 70% of executive leadership in corporations are conservative, according to research done by Harvard University in 2022. Generally speaking, being more educated makes you more likely to be a liberal. The exception to this rule appears to be MBAs, who will end up having a lot of money personally, and managing companies that have a lot of money. Voting conservative is in their interest. Given how friendly conservatives are to the wealthy, how do they pull off the bait-and-switch to paint themselves as supporters of the working class?

First off, they have to because you can't win elections if only rich people vote for you. Second, there are a handful of highly visible liberal-dominated industries like tech, media, and education. However, the companies that do almost everything else are led by conservative MBAs. Third, it *feels* like companies are liberal because of how "woke" almost every company is. If 70% of MBAs are conservative, and MBAs run companies, why do so many companies look liberal? Because as a fiduciary representative of a corporation, the MBA manager's job is to maximize the value of the company, not to use the company as a tool to spread her personal beliefs.

Most companies just want to play it safe and not get singled out for anything. In an environment where every other company stands with Black Lives Matter, are you going to be the only one in your industry that doesn't? When they ask why you didn't, what are you going to say? All of a sudden, you're known as a racist company, whether it's true or not.

Even if you personally are conservative and don't like BLM, to make the most money, it's probably best not to become the target of a scandal, justified or unjustified. While you're trying to explain your innocence, you just look guilty. The public doesn't have the attention span to appreciate nuanced arguments and data anyway.

MBAs, like most people, tend to be risk-averse. If they take a bold stance and it doesn't work out in the short to medium term, they are likely going to get fired. If they blend in with everyone else, even if they fail with everyone, they will still probably keep their jobs. This is why companies so often follow each other. It's the safest thing to do.

Winning the working class is key to winning elections. In order to do this, we need to make as few enemies as possible. We don't need to be "against" entire groups of people. I must say, you've got to be talented to take a term like "inclusion," and make it feel tribal; unfortunately, we pulled it off.

Inclusion is good, but we need to try again, inclusion 2.0. This time, let's not tie the concept of inclusion to divisive identity politics. The only group of people we should be against, are people with bad policy ideas. Other than that, everyone should feel equal, and welcome. If we make an effort to be truly inclusive, I believe we'd have a strong case that we're the lesser of two evils for independents like Jack and Jill.

9. Problems of Scale

"And those who were seen dancing were thought to be insane by those who could not hear the music."
– Friedrich Nietzsche

♫ Dancing in the Moonlight | King Harvest

Tens of thousands of migrants are crossing the southern border every week, with no end in sight. Criminals are moving into vacant properties, forcing homeowners to spend months evicting them. Social Security reserves are projected to run out in 2033. Peace between major powers seems to be coming to an end. These issues are concerning to most Americans on both sides of the aisle. Though the subject matter of each issue is distinct, they are all problems of scale.

Squatters

The criminals who maliciously move into vacant homes and then claim to be tenants are colloquially called *squatters*. Their goal is simple—to live rent-free until the owner is able to force them out through the legal system. Common sense tells us that they shouldn't be able to do this. The fact that they can appears to be a hole in the system so large that it had to have been made by either a madman or a fool.

Usually, when something seems incredibly and obviously stupid, there is more to the story. There aren't many Bobs in the world. Instead of jumping to the conclusion that our government is made of fools, and staying there, I decided to find out what the fools were thinking.

When you see a homeowner put in handcuffs and forced into the back of a police car because she changed the locks on her own property, it looks bad. What you're seeing is wrong; it's hard to argue otherwise. Why does the squatter, the criminal, get to win?

They win because individual police officers shouldn't have the authority to decide, in the moment, who has the right to live in a particular property. Officers aren't experts in rental contracts. Even if they were, you can't expect both parties to have all of the paperwork prepared when you show up. We don't want Officer Jared in a parking lot at eight o'clock at night trying to determine whether or not the lease the squatter printed is real.

If police could kick squatters out, squatters could print fake deeds, claim the owner is a squatter, then kick them out of their own home with the government's help. Landlords could claim that a legitimate tenant who paid rent three months in advance is a squatter. They could easily prove to the police that they are the owner, have the tenant forcibly removed, then re-rent the property while pocketing the tenant's rent money. The current squatter situation doesn't feel right, but letting individual policemen make the decision doesn't feel right either.

The best way to find out who should live in a property with a high degree of certainty, is through the courts. At trial, there is a judge who is trained in these disputes, and both sides can present their best evidence with legal counsel. The downside is that this is a lengthy and expensive process.

When it's not common knowledge that you can squat in vacant properties to live rent-free for months, it rarely happens, so it's not a societal problem. When videos go viral on social media explaining precisely how it's done, the crime becomes more popular. This bogs down the legal system, making it take even longer to remove squatters. The more squatters there are, the more attractive squatting becomes.

Most of the squatter laws across the country aren't new; what's new is the large quantity of criminals looking to abuse the laws. At this scale, it is a societal problem that needs to be fixed. However, the people who wrote the initial laws weren't imbeciles, nor were they trying to destroy the country.

Migrants

Referring to Mexican migrants, President Trump infamously said, "They are bringing drugs, they are bringing crime, they are rapists … and some, I assume, are good people." Though most of us don't approve of blanket rape accusations against large groups of people, it sends a clear emotional message that he's against the migrants at the southern border. As you watch liberals criticize Trump's callousness, it's understandable to arrive at the conclusion that Republicans are against illegal immigration, and Democrats support illegal immigration.

It feels like we Democrats support illegal immigration, but is it true? Immigrant advocacy groups were very upset with President Obama, calling him "deporter in chief" due to the number of deportations executed by his administration. On January 2, 2024, Republican Governor Ron DeSantis said, "Trump promised the largest deportations in history … He deported less, believe it or not, than Barack Obama even did." Though DeSantis's point was that Trump deported less than Obama, a more complete statement is that every president deported less than Obama. We'll see if that remains true once Biden's numbers come in.

For the sake of transparency, there are some disputes related to the evolving definition of the term "deportation" before and after the presidency of George W. Bush. These disputes about what constitutes a deportation can make the question of whether or not Obama deported the most in history a bit unclear. Details like these are why you have to be careful, even with statistics.

Regardless of the technicalities around which activities constitute a deportation, DeSantis was right. Obama deported more than Trump. The problem is, your average voter doesn't know a single deportation statistic, let alone how the definition of "deportation" changed over time, or each president's numbers relative to each other. Voters do know that Trump called them names, and presume that he must be the tough one.

We Democrats will respect you as a human being, and then deport you. We don't have to insult you while we enforce the law. "Top of the morning! Hope you're doing quite well. It's time to go." It reminds me of how I was disciplined when I was growing up. My parents didn't feel the need to raise their voices with me. Discipline was tough, but it wasn't angry.

Deportation statistics aside, we still have a problem at the southern border. Instead of competing for who can generate the best migrant insults, let's try to understand the problem, so we can solve it. This brings us to the concepts of refugees and asylees. Both are people seeking entry into the United States as a means of fleeing persecution. Refugees apply remotely; asylees apply after making the journey to the United States.

Problems of Scale

There is an annual target cap on the number of refugees we accept into the country. This is normally in the tens of thousands per year, but lately it has been just above one hundred thousand. The refugee system makes sense. There is a limit on how many we accept, and they're required to follow formal processes. Though we plan to grant one hundred thousand refugees entry into the United States per year, we sometimes see more than double that number per month at the southern border.

There is a cap on the number of refugees per year, but the number of people permitted to seek asylum is unlimited. Though there is no cap, asylum seekers are still required to follow a formal process. They have to explain why they are seeking asylum in a "credible fear interview," then have their case heard by a judge to determine whether or not asylum will be granted. If they fail the credible fear interview, they will be deported without getting to see a judge.

There is a cap on refugees, why isn't there a cap on asylum seekers? For starters, capping the number of asylees would violate international law. That's good to know, but laws aren't reasons; laws are laws. Suppose there is an atrocity occurring at the scale of Nazi Germany's persecution of Jewish people. If a Jewish family managed to escape after being sent to a concentration camp, it would feel quite bad to deport them back into the heart of Germany. If we did, and that family was subsequently killed, some of that blood would be on our hands.

Since we'd rather not be in the business of sending Jews back to Nazi Germany, we want to hear every case. It would be a shame to go, "Yes, you are clearly Jewish, fleeing the Nazis. Unfortunately, our quota this year was sixty-five thousand, so we'll have to send you back. Good luck to you and your family."

I used the Nazi example to communicate clearly why we don't feel comfortable deporting people to their deaths. Today, migrants at our southern border aren't fleeing Nazis, obviously. Many of them are fleeing persecution from countries in South America like Venezuela, Guatemala, and Honduras.

The people I'm referring to above are legitimate asylum seekers fleeing persecution. Intermingled among them are people looking to game the system in order to enter the United States. Many of them are rejected before they even get to apply for asylum, by failing the credible fear interview. The rest will have their day in court.

It's similar to the squatter situation; the large quantity of both legitimate asylum seekers and criminal opportunists bogs down our legal system. It can sometimes take over a year for them to see a judge. Until then, they are allowed to stay in the United States. These long processing times make the system even more attractive to the opportunists looking to take advantage of it.

This brings me to a broad pattern I've recognized among Democrats and Republicans. Democrats tend to assume the best; Republicans tend to assume the worst. Conservatives look at the masses at the southern border, and think about Mexican drug dealers looking to get rich selling fentanyl to our youth. Liberals look at them, and see families like ours fleeing for their lives. On the trans issue, Democrats think of regular trans people just trying to live with respect and not be bothered. Republicans think of male criminals who claim to be transwomen so they can go to female prisons and live like kings. They think of the unremarkable male athlete who realizes that as a transwoman, she will become remarkable again.

All of those people exist. If you have a strong emphasis on the negative side, like conservatives, they deserve scorn, or worse. If you have a strong emphasis on the positive side, like liberals, they deserve respect, and should be protected. Protecting families who are in danger of torture or murder is honorable. Protecting the drug dealers who sell death to young people makes conservatives turn to conspiracy theories.

Instead of looking at everything like it's good, or everything like it's bad, we should be trying to find ways to keep the good and dispose of the bad. As Democrats, we can reduce tribalism by simply admitting that there are bad sides to the trans and immigration issues. If we make it clear that we understand their concerns, conservatives will be more open to understanding our concerns. I believe President Bill Clinton did a good job with this in his 1995 State of the Union speech.

> "We are a nation of immigrants, but we are also a nation of laws. It is wrong, and ultimately self-defeating, for a nation of immigrants to permit the kind of abuse of our immigration laws we have seen in recent years, and we must do more to stop it."
>
> – Bill Clinton

Clinton communicates respect for immigrants while recognizing that it's possible for bad actors to abuse our laws. Conservatives don't have to jump to conspiracy theories, and we don't have to call them bigots. Together, we can try to preserve the spirit of our laws while making them less abusable by bad actors.

Once liberals and conservatives have established mutual respect, the rest is a matter of policy. Biden tried to reject more asylees before they enter the legal system by requiring them to apply for asylum in countries they had to pass through in order to get to the United States. This way they couldn't use asylum as an excuse to come here; they would have had to have gotten rejected from each country along the way first. Biden also tried to automatically reject anyone who crossed the border without getting processed through an official port of entry. Both of those ideas seem reasonable to me.

Biden's efforts above were rejected by a Californian judge who claimed that his administration's actions violated federal law, which states that anyone on US soil can request asylum, no matter how they arrived. The same judge blocked a similar measure from the Trump administration. Biden was blocked, Trump was blocked; that's what I like to see. Fair, non-partisan treatment from the legal system. Also, based on the law, I can't argue that the judge was wrong. That means our congressmen need to have some tough legislative conversations about the asylum process. Speaking of tough conversations, the next problem of scale we'll discuss is Social Security.

Social Security

Few people have the courage to take a decidedly unpopular stance in public, especially when they have something to lose. Conservative commentator Ben Shapiro took such a stance on Social Security. Though I don't agree with the details of his recommendations, I commend his willingness to talk about it. Though I suppose I shouldn't be surprised at his candor; this is the man known for repeating the phrase, "Facts don't care about your feelings."

What's the problem with Social Security anyway? Math. Social Security is a math problem. One that doesn't add up. At the top of the chapter, I mentioned that the Social Security reserve is projected to run out in 2033. Let's unpack what that means with a brief explanation of how Social Security works.

Working people pay Social Security taxes on their income. The total is 12.4%. Half comes from the employee, and half comes from the employer. To be eligible for Social Security benefits, you must have paid Social Security taxes for at least ten years, and be at least sixty-two years old. The longer you delay receiving Social Security benefits, and the higher your income, the larger your Social Security checks will be. For example, if you wait until seventy to receive Social Security benefits, you will get more money per check than if you started receiving benefits at sixty-five.

Social Security provides monthly income for the rest of your life. There are two important variables in the previous sentence. The dollar amount of the monthly income, and how long the rest of your life is. The larger the Social Security checks, and the longer you live while receiving Social Security benefits, the greater the cost to society.

Another important variable that we often don't think about is the population age distribution. If there are plenty of young workers paying Social Security taxes, and few retirees receiving benefits, you have stability. If there are plenty of retirees receiving benefits, and few workers paying into the system, you have math problems.

Considering all of our variables, the worst-case scenario is a population distribution heavily weighted toward elderly people who have a long life expectancy and receive large monthly benefits. With the arguable exception of large benefits, the worst-case scenario is our current reality.

Excluding infant mortality and other causes of preadult death, people are living two to five years longer on average, depending on sex, than they were in 1940. It's great that people are living longer, but it makes Social Security less sustainable. The impact of life expectancy is significant, but a more influential factor is the population distribution. In 1960, there were 5.1 people paying into the system for each retiree receiving benefits. In 2022, there were only 2.8 people supporting each retiree. So today, less than three people are responsible for supporting the same number of retirees that more than five people used to support, and those retirees are living two to five years longer.

The Social Security reserve I mentioned was built up over time because the government collected more in Social Security taxes than it paid out in benefits. The government invests and earns interest on this money. This is the ideal process. The government collects a little more than it pays out, and over time it builds up a safety reserve of cash it can dip into to cover years when it doesn't collect enough in taxes to fund benefits.

However, since 2010, we've been paying out more in Social Security benefits than we've been collecting in taxes. Initially, we tapped into the interest income generated from the reserve fund to cover the gap. Now, the fund doesn't generate enough interest, so we're tapping into the principal to cover the gap. Once you start spending the principal, it generates less interest, and it's a downward spiral to zero from there. This spiral is projected to end in 2033. At that point, there will only be the current year's Social Security taxes available to fund benefits. With no reserves to tap into, there would only be enough money to cover approximately 80% of our Social Security commitments.

It's clear that Social Security isn't sustainable. Not only is it clear now, it has been clear for a long time. Social Security policy was a significant topic of debate in the 2000 presidential race between Al Gore and George W. Bush. We know the current size of the reserve, the population distribution, birth rates, long-term GDP growth rates, and our inflation targets. Our predictions aren't perfect, but we've known for decades that Social Security reserves would run out in the first half of the century.

It's similar to climate change. It's happening slowly. We see it coming, but people won't take it seriously until their benefits are cut by 20%. Then they'll be surprised. Remember, that 20% cut isn't the end; it's just the beginning, for retirees in 2033. What about young people paying into the system today, expecting to receive benefits in the 2060s? Good luck; hope you'll be able to afford a nice air conditioner.

I don't claim to have the wisdom or experience necessary to dictate solutions to these problems of scale. I can, however, point out the obvious variables we have control over. For Social Security, we don't control the population distribution or birth rates. We can either raise taxes, increase the retirement age, cut benefits, or end the program entirely. For the southern border, we can create more reasons to reject migrants before they enter the court system, find ways to shorten wait times to see a judge, implement a cap on the number of asylees, or break international law and end the asylum program altogether. For squatters, people can find ways to abuse the system regardless of whether disputes are settled through housing courts or fast-tracked through law enforcement. Perhaps we should add tougher criminal penalties for those we can prove were acting maliciously, beyond a reasonable doubt.

Social Security, asylum, and housing courts are good ideas fundamentally. However, problems of scale demand that we put our thinking caps on. That is, if we're more interested in solving problems than complaining about them. We need to be prepared to have tough conversations, like Ben Shapiro. Tough, but in good faith.

Common Interests

Squatters, the southern border, and Social Security are problems of scale within the scope of the United States. Common interest is a problem of scale that can be broad enough to encompass foreign policy, or narrow enough to fit within the family unit. Tribalism tends to express itself in groups united by common interests.

The irony is that common interests are both causes of and solutions to tribalism. Tribalism occurs when groups united by common interests have competitive interests with each other. The consequences are bias, groupthink, extremism, hatred, etc. If the competing groups are able to find common interests with each other, there would only be one group. At this level of scale, competitive interests would be gone, along with most of the negative elements of tribalism. Though if you increase the scale, this newly combined group could find another group to compete with, birthing a broader layer of tribalism.

The economic theories of capitalism and socialism draw an interesting parallel between competitive interests, and common interests, respectively. Though, it's worth noting that Adam Smith, the economist known as the father of capitalism, argued that competitive interests in a free market serve the common interest indirectly.

Within our households, most of us, including fiscal conservatives, support socialism—communal ownership of resources. In the familial context, your value isn't determined by the marketplace. As long as no one is a glutton, there's no need to keep detailed accounting of the cookie jar's inventory.

Even in church, conservatives appreciate the beauty of socialism. A community of neighbors with common values and interests coming together to support each other. Paying tithes not to enrich celebrity preachers, but to fund programs that benefit the entire congregation. To have a common pool of resources that helps members who have fallen upon hard times. Knowing that there is a village behind you that has your back. Most of us would agree, this picture doesn't need to be stained by the mark of capitalism.

Socialism in the government makes conservatives tremble in their boots. Though, in my conversations with them, they tend to like socialism they benefit from. Popular socialist policies among conservatives include but are not limited to Social Security, Medicare, and free public education.

On election day, 2020, I spoke with a group of conservative student activists at the Ohio State University. I asked them who their favorite Democrat was. To my surprise, the most popular by far was Andrew Yang. Given that conservatives are supposed to want "small government," I was curious about why they liked Yang so much. Yang's flagship policy was universal basic income (UBI). If implemented, it would be one of the largest government programs in history.

When I asked them how they reconciled supporting UBI and small government at the same time, this was their response. "We'd rather support a conservative and not have universal basic income at all. However, if we are going to have social programs, I'd rather them be fair and apply to everyone, instead of only helping certain people, like welfare."

My general takeaway from that conversation was the following. The more a given socialist policy appears to be in your interest, the more likely you are to support it. Ironically, this reminds me of capitalism, where the fundamental assumption is that people are self-interested. Perhaps if you follow a truly free capitalistic market to its end, the people will create a government and proceed to implement socialist programs that they think will be in their interest.

Socialism at home, fantastic. Socialism in church, great. Socialism for public schools, parts of health care, and Social Security, good. Socialism for all business, horrible. Regardless of whether or not it's good for society, you can sell socialism to capitalists if you convince them that it's in their interest. Conservatives don't like big government programs, but they do like bigger ones.

Thinking back on the campus conversation, I realize that it became less tribal once we began talking about UBI. As we discussed briefly in chapter 4, I'm personally not a fan of UBI right now. It seems wasteful to collect a bunch of taxes to help everyone, including those who don't need help. I'd rather collect less taxes and help those who need it, while providing incentives for them to help themselves. Targeted support is more economically efficient, but it emphasizes competitive interests between groups of citizens. UBI, in contrast, emphasizes common interests, and was able to bring young conservatives to the table.

It's natural for humans to think in terms of the common interest at small scales, and competitive interests at large scales. To reduce tribalism, we may need to find ways to scale the common interest. This is difficult, because it's unnatural. The status quo, tribalism at scale, is natural.

If we had a pressing reason to operate in the realm of the common interest at scale, like a hostile alien civilization, we could do it. Faced with enemy spaceships, we wouldn't have time for identity politics at the local, national, or international levels. No need to contrast the intersectional analyses of Black trans people and cisgender White males. No need for well-to-do white-collar workers in the city to look down on rural rednecks in the back of pickup trucks, or vice versa. Most border disputes wouldn't seem very

Problems of Scale

important anymore. The US, Israel, Iran, Hamas, NATO, Russia, and China would coordinate to fire missiles together, instead of at each other. Imminent doom may be just what it takes to create the world imagined by John Lennon. Bittersweet, but if we're going to go out, I'd rather go out together.

If we were able to pull off a miracle and repel the alien invaders, I fear it wouldn't be long before we got back to debating the superiority of the blond-haired, blue-eyed Aryan race. Within a couple of decades, I wouldn't be surprised if we reverse-engineered the alien military technology, and started using it on each other.

Though I'm loath to admit it, self-interest may simply be too powerful to fight. Common interest works when the common interest and self-interests are aligned. For example, it's in our common interest to responsibly manage climate change. It's in our self-interest to live life to the fullest, and hope someone else solves the problem.

When we successfully align common and competitive interests, it's usually on a small scale, like within the family. I don't know the answer, but this is the question—how can we align competitive interests with the common interest, at scale?

10. Welcome to the Jungle

*"This advice would not be good if men were good,
but they are not ..."*
– Niccolò Machiavelli

♪ Streets is Watching | Jay-Z

Niccolò Machiavelli was an Italian statesman and philosopher whose work was so influential that his last name has become an adjective. Machiavellianism, as they say, is used to describe his political philosophy, most famously outlined in his book *The Prince*. Though few are aware of the details of his arguments, Machiavellianism is colloquially referred to as a worldview that is selfish and amoral. Consequently, it usually comes with a negative, borderline psychopathic connotation. Regardless of how you feel about it, the Machiavellian context of viewing the world is a real one. Perhaps the most real, when you are faced with a true Machiavellian.

In chapter 6 of this book, we explored the concept of the "ideal" society. This is the society that is as good as it can possibly be, within the limits of human nature. Those limits are important, as it keeps us from wishful thinking ourselves into ideals that don't work. Machiavellianism reminds me of capitalism. It is brutally honest about accepting human nature, and gives no illusions that it cares about being good. That's why it works.

We liberals want to be good. Our hearts are in the right places. Though I occasionally disagree with our implementation details, I rarely feel the need to question our motives. We're sensitive. We try to protect people from getting their feelings hurt. We're highly judgmental of people we feel aren't good enough. Even me personally, I pride myself on being a man of honor. I love societal contexts that involve justice, fairness, peace, reason, and understanding. I want to live in this pristine world. Our institutions and cultures attempt to create this world for us. As beautiful as this world may be, the truth is we're in the jungle, and Machiavelli is honest about it. Understanding the truth in Machiavellianism can help us remain grounded in reality while pursuing our ideals.

Good Men

After our journeys through individual and societal contexts, it should be clear that most people aren't as good as they believe they are. It hopefully is also clear that most people do sincerely believe that they are good. Even if you're not as good as you think you are, it's OK; at least you value goodness.

Per our coverage of the math tryouts, if you have a disagreement in a z-length problem on part j, it's best to find the point of divergence and start there. For example, you may agree on a and b, but start to disagree on c, which continues through to j. Valuing goodness generally is perhaps the most basic fundamental agreement there can be. If we can start there as step a, at least we have something to work with. For someone who doesn't value goodness at all, arguing with them about moral concerns is often a waste of breath.

I believe there are four types of people based on how they feel about "goodness" and "honor." Goodness is difficult to define, so I won't. For this exercise it only matters that the person values goodness, whatever that means to them. I define honor as a person's willingness to sacrifice for goodness when it is inconvenient for them. I'm going to set up a real-life scenario to illustrate the different combinations.

There is a promotion available at your company. Your coworker, Amy, clearly deserves it more than anyone else. She's the most competent and works the hardest. The high-ups at the company aren't aware of Amy's unique excellence as an employee. You have the same chance of getting the promotion as Amy does if you apply for it. The company will have more success if she gets the promotion than if you do. Do you apply for the promotion?

- James: If you ask James, he will tell you he values fairness. However, if he has the opportunity to win the promotion, he's going to go for it, even though he knows he's not the best for the job.

- Tina: Tina values fairness. She decides not to compete with Amy for the promotion because she knows Amy deserves it, at personal cost to herself.

- Joan: Joan doesn't care about fairness at all. Joan cares about Joan because she is Joan. It doesn't need to get more complicated than that. Joan will compete with Amy without remorse.

- Vinnie: Vinnie delights in the suffering of others. Vinnie will attempt to plant evidence to get Amy fired. If he succeeds and feels safe to do so, he'll let Amy know he was behind it so she's aware of his victory over her.

People like James, Tina, Joan, and Vinnie exist. However, they don't exist at the same rates. They are listed below in what I believe to be popularity order.

- James: Values goodness, low in honor
- Tina: Values goodness, high in honor
- Joan: Doesn't value goodness, has no honor
- Vinnie: Values evil, has no honor

Most of us are like James; we try to do good things, unless it conflicts with our self-interest. Tina is the ideal we want in society, but most of us are still working toward it. Joan is what I would describe as a psychopath. Psychopaths aren't interested in "good" for others unless they get something out of it. Note that this doesn't make them evil. Not valuing good is far from valuing evil. Psychopaths like Joan are about 1% of the general population. Evil people like Vinnie are much rarer than psychopaths, thankfully. However, some of them are still out there; I hope you don't cross paths with them.

It's important to note how common James and Tina are compared to Joan and Vinnie. A common mistake we make is to say things like, "They're all terrible people," as if a majority of any large group of people consists of Joans and Vinnies. Could there be a small group of Joans and Vinnies working together? Sure, but as the group grows larger than a handful, the odds decline precipitously.

The comparison between James and Joan is an interesting one. Psychopaths can blend in because they usually aren't evil, and they often make the same decisions as a regular person who is low in honor. Though their actions are often similar, Joan is an entirely different animal. If James were raised in a different context, he could end up very close to Joan, or he could end up like Tina. In contrast, Joan is most likely just going to be Joan, regardless of her context. What's the difference?

With Joan, you can't even agree on step *a* of morality, which is a goal to pursue goodness. Discussing a moral question with someone who doesn't care about goodness, is like arguing rationally with someone who doesn't appreciate logic. If you can't agree at the most fundamental level, then progress is practically impossible.

James can be worked with, Joan cannot. A poorly civilized James may be difficult to distinguish from Joan based on their actions. Yet there is a real, fundamental difference between the two. James and Tina are on a spectrum. Joan is simply missing something that most other humans have. Very few people are as intellectually vacuous as Bob from the math tryouts. Likewise, very few people are as morally vacuous as Joan or Vinnie. If you think any large group of people are like them, you're almost certainly wrong. Note that this is based on their definition of good, not yours.

Since most of us are somewhere between James and Tina, we can play the game of civilization, treating each other as generally good actors we can expect won't surprise us with anything horrible. However, Joan and Vinnie can force us out of our game and into the jungle. We can't force them into civilization.

When it comes to leading organizations like an ideal prince, Machiavelli argues that though people like to see their leaders as good, what they like more are results. If a leader is delivering results to her organization and making its members better off, the people she is leading will likely find an excuse for any "bad" things she did.

It's arguably against the law to be a good leader of a company. Managers of corporations have something called a *fiduciary duty* to the shareholders. Shareholders are the owners of the company, but they don't manage it day to day. Employees of the company like the CEO and the rest of the executive leadership team manage it. It is their duty to act in the interest of the shareholders. In other words, it's their job to maximize the value of the shares of the company. If they neglect this responsibility, it is called a *breach of fiduciary duty*, which they can be sued for.

Suppose Alana is a restaurant owner and she hired Dan as a manager. At the end of the week, Dan took all of the money Alana's restaurant made, as well as its food, and donated it to charity. He thought it was a good thing to do. Though it may have been the most "good" use of the company's resources, you probably would be pretty unhappy if you were Alana. Alana could sue Dan for breach of fiduciary duty to get compensated for her company's assets that he gave away.

Giving away all of a company's assets to charity is an extreme example. Fundamentally, if the managers of a corporation are doing anything other than maximizing shareholder value, they are doing it wrong. If this is done egregiously, they open themselves up to a lawsuit. This means that their job is practically to be Joan.

They aren't leading the company to make the world a better place. They aren't here to improve the United States. Employees aren't members of a family. They are expenses to be minimized and automated away whenever possible, insofar as it doesn't hurt competitive viability and long-term growth. They are running the company to make money for its owners. It's not the CEO's job to worry about the safety of the city's water supply. That's the government's job.

The only reason to justify the CEO being "good," is if the "good" reputation of the company will improve the brand enough to result in greater profits for the company in the long run. This is why so many companies led by conservatives still look liberal. If conservative leaders use the companies they run to voice their personal politics, it would be a breach of fiduciary duty. It's not their job to play politics. It's their job to maximize shareholder value.

In a job where being "good" is a distraction, Joan might actually be better suited for it than Tina or James. This is likely why there is a higher rate of psychopathy in CEOs than in the general population. Still a minority, perhaps 4%–10% of CEOs display psychopathic traits. James as a CEO may feel pressure to think like Joan for his career, even if that's not how he is personally.

People like Joan are not only valuable in the corporate world, but also in government. Leaders who the people believe will accomplish great things for them will rise to the top. The important part of the previous sentence is "for them." Just as it is not the CEO's job to worry about the city's water supply, it's not the leader of a given nation's job to worry about people in other nations. It's not that leader's job to worry about the global environment. Caring too much about other people is a distraction from taking care of your own people. It's similar to a breach of fiduciary duty, but in a government context instead of a corporate one.

Even if the politician does some bad things, as long as it works out in the end, their people will make up an excuse for it. If the leader does something "good," and it doesn't get results the people want, they are in trouble. I don't like leaders like Joan, but that doesn't mean they are ineffective. Populist movements on both sides of the aisle are the people's way of holding their leaders to account for not acting enough in their interest.

Unfortunately, thinking like a Machiavellian is practically in the job description for our leaders. Most of them have only the interest of their people in mind. If they didn't, their people would choose a different leader. But what happens when you have leaders who only care about their people, and no one cares about good for others? What happens when a majority of leaders are either people like Joan or people like James trying to behave like Joan? You get conflict. You certainly get conflict when Machiavellians feel it will benefit them. I fear that this may be a situation that is unavoidable for humans. I don't believe it has to be, but it very well may be. If we can't figure out how to value "good" for people outside of our groups, it could be the end of us.

Law, Biden, Citizen

Crime is a hot-button issue that generates a lot of fear, gun sales, and votes. Conservatives attempt to paint themselves as the "law and order" party. While doing so, we liberals are often implicitly or explicitly portrayed as an unlawful disorder party. As this narrative grows, its believers fear not only criminals, but Democrats.

Let's examine the 95th percentile scared conservative, Zane. His spidey senses are always tingling. His confidence level is somewhere between Scooby Doo and Courage the Cowardly Dog, but he wears a mean scowl and he's armed to the teeth. He's concerned that birds on power lines are actually government drones spying on him. Zane thinks Bill Gates wants to listen to his conversations on the telephone. He's worried about serial killers, car thefts, fentanyl, the deep state, sex trafficking, and most of all, the left. He's afraid of almost everything; some concerns are more valid than others. However, even for Zane, there is one thing I'm willing to bet he's not concerned about. The possibility of a criminal stealing his primary residence.

Zane may be concerned about home invaders attempting to harm his family or steal his property. He may worry about the possibility of squatters moving into a vacant property and claiming to be tenants. However, he's not likely concerned about a criminal forcing him out of his home at gunpoint and claiming to own it because might makes right. This type of crime practically never happens in the United States. It's so rare, I don't even know if there is a name for it. Homes are often worth hundreds of thousands of dollars. The incentive is strong, yet no one steals any. Why?

The answer is simple: It's because of law enforcement. Particularly, the "enforcement" part. What is a law with no enforcement to a Machiavellian? A suggestion. No one steals homes because it's practically impossible to. If an armed group of criminals seized a residence, within twenty-four hours they'd almost certainly be in handcuffs.

I understand that this line of inquiry doesn't feel like groundbreaking analysis. It isn't. I'm just trying to emphasize how important law enforcement is. We need the police. Get rid of the police, and stealing homes worth six figures becomes a highly lucrative criminal enterprise. It would be much more attractive than conducting smash-and-grabs at retailers, or selling illicit drugs.

Hopefully we all can agree that we need law enforcement to prevent groups of thugs from commandeering private properties. What happens when we expand the scope, and the "thugs" who want to steal property are soldiers from another nation? At scale of nations, as opposed to neighborhoods, the incentive for stealing properties is perhaps even larger. However, there is no police.

If an individual home is worth six figures, how much is a neighborhood worth? The real estate in a single city can be worth over $100 billion. Consider what a state or province is worth, what an entire country is worth. We're talking gargantuan amounts of money, and that's just the real estate value. If you can steal an entire country's worth of real estate, you can steal their companies too. Add the value of public and private enterprises to the value of the real estate, and we're talking about an astronomical amount of money. This doesn't even count the strategic military benefits, including the ability to draft new soldiers from the land you just conquered.

The more countries you steal, the greater your military power becomes, which makes stealing more countries even easier. The theft of nations is perhaps the best business I can imagine if you aren't restricted by morals, and you have the power to accomplish it. Perhaps that's why it happens so often in history.

Now that we've examined the true value of militaristic aggression, I'd like to pose a question. Why are so many of us comfortable without police? My conservative friends are often concerned about law enforcement when it's poor thieves in the local neighborhood, but they are comfortable with military aggressors in the global neighborhood. My liberal friends are often concerned about law and order in the global neighborhood, but are too lax in the local one. In my opinion, the best option for our long-run safety is to support law and order in both contexts, local and global.

One of the biggest complaints I see about Biden, other than his age, is his administration's foreign policy positions. The Biden administration stands steadfast in support of its allies including non-NATO members like Israel, Ukraine, and Taiwan. Conservatives don't want us helping other nations when we have problems at home. "America first, we don't need to be the global police," they say.

To some extent they are correct. We have neither the means nor the authority to act as "the police" in a global context. "The police" is a law enforcement institution that needs to be more powerful than any group of bad actors within its jurisdiction. At the current moment, no such institution exists, and even if it did, it would be difficult to manage and trust. So there will be no global police. The best we can do is participate in something like a global neighborhood watch.

NATO is the large, formal neighborhood watch. Everyone is better off with the confidence that we have each other's backs. The key word in the previous sentence is "confidence." It's mandatory to be able to call 911 and have someone on the other end of the phone. Participating in the global neighborhood watch is not mandatory. If we signal hesitance, reluctance, or division, it sends a message to criminals who want to test our watch, as well as to fellow members of the watch. Like financial markets, military alliances can crumble quickly when confidence is lost, especially when under pressure.

Conservatives see the Biden administration's steadfast support of our allies as some globalist agenda that doesn't have the interest of Americans at heart. In reality, he's keeping the neighborhood watch as strong as possible by not folding under pressure. Though Ukraine, Israel, and Taiwan aren't NATO members, we're still committed to their support. This should give NATO members assurance that we have their backs, as well as other non-NATO allies like Japan and Australia.

We shouldn't try to be the global police. However, we should be a model citizen in the global neighborhood. The neighborhood watch is essential if we want to protect ourselves from criminals stealing our homes. The watch doesn't mean anything if we're only committed to it when our personal property is at risk. Furthermore, if we wait until the problem is at our doorstep, it will likely be too late. This is because if we let bad actors take over the neighborhood, they will be too large to resist. This almost happened with Nazi Germany in World War II.

Intuitively, it appears to be against our Machiavellian interest to support foreign nations. However, smart Machiavellians understand that it's in our interest to have friends. You don't have to care about our allies morally, but the least you could do is be a smart Machiavellian.

Superior Force

At any time, anywhere, anybody can choose to force you into the jungle. The option is always on the table. Civilized people don't often consider this option, but it is ever present nonetheless.

Imagine Freddy is in a room listening to the CEO of his organization give a speech. The CEO is the boss, right? He has authority over everyone else at the company, besides the board of directors. If Freddy decides to walk next to the CEO, pull out a knife and hold it to his neck, who is the boss now? Freddy has just forced the entire room into the jungle. The entire system of laws, best practices, common decency, and corporate hierarchy just got thrown out the window and ignored. Right now, Freddy is the boss. He will remain the boss until he is met with a superior force. Then we can go back to our game of civilization.

Suppose Freddy is attracted to his neighbor Jason's wife. Jason is much larger than Freddy and in better shape, so Freddy suspects he can't win a fair fight. He knocks on Jason's door, and creates some excuse to get invited in for a moment. When Jason turns his back, Freddy attacks him with a hammer, knocking him unconscious. Now if Freddy is more powerful than Jason's wife, he can do as he pleases with her until he is met with a superior force.

I put Freddy in highly charged and disturbing situations because that's what the worst consequences of foreign policy look like, but at scale. It's not pleasant to think about, but it is all too real. War. War comes with death obviously. It often comes with other evils like torture, slavery, and sexual assault. Though it's not common in modern armed conflicts, intentional mass rape as a fear tactic is an option some aggressors choose to employ. It's uncomfortable to read this. I'm uncomfortable writing it, but suffering doesn't go away when we close our eyes. These are the stakes of international relations, diplomacy, war, extremism, and tribalism.

David French is a Harvard-educated lawyer, veteran, professor, and writer. He was a guest on Sam Harris's podcast where they discussed ideas from French's book *Divided We Fall*. It was a great conversation. I encourage you to look it up and listen to it if you enjoy podcasts. There were two ideas from that conversation that stood out to me.

The first idea was how it wasn't policies but grievances that fueled the violence between Shia and Sunni Muslims in Iraq. French noted that from a policy perspective, things like religious tolerance for each other and dividing oil revenues were solvable. What was much more difficult to solve, were the real grievances they had. You could talk to a Shia militant and he would have a truly horrible experience that justifies his hatred of the Sunni. Something like a bombing that decimated his brother's body so badly he only survived a few months in extreme pain before succumbing to his wounds. Then he would talk to a Sunni militant, and they would have a story that was similarly brutal.

Can you blame them for hating the people who committed atrocities against their loved ones? I can't. Imagine just 1% of Sunni and 1% of Shia are extremists who commit acts of violence against each other. Picking randomly here, a Sunni extremist commits an atrocity that kills ten innocent Shia Muslims. Would you be surprised if that darkness spreads, increasing the rate of Shia extremists to 1.5%? Then the Shia commit an atrocity that kills ten innocent Sunni Muslims. The cycle grows and perpetuates itself, understandably so.

Policies are policies. We can sit back like Greek philosophers and debate the ideal society. But let us watch our loved ones struggle and die due to the aggression of our enemies, and then ask how much we feel like pretending to be scholars. At the time of writing this in October of 2023, Hamas recently attacked Israel, causing Israeli prime minister Benjamin Netanyahu to declare war.

Regardless of your position on the broader Israeli-Palestinian conflict, you can't accept terrorism and the intentional killing of innocent people, including children. In my view, it's optimal to be against Hamas, but that is not the same as being against the Palestinians, most of whom are innocent people. To be clear, I believe that everyone should be against Hamas even if you are pro-Palestinian.

Hamas's military leader Mohammed Deif is known as "the guest," because he sleeps in a different location every night to avoid assassination by the Israelis. He has been injured multiple times, but he hasn't been killed yet. In addition to "the guest," they also call him the "cat with nine lives," due to his history of surviving multiple close calls.

In 2014, his wife and one of his children died in an Israeli military strike that was intended to kill him. I don't have sympathy for Deif, but understand that if you injure a man, kill his wife, and kill his child, you're going to have a real problem on your hands. Deif was a terrorist before he lost his family, but now he's a terrorist with real grievances. It's his fault for being a terrorist. Regardless of fault, for someone in that frame of mind, I wouldn't be surprised by violence and barbarism.

The second idea that stood out from the conversation between

Sam Harris and David French, was how extremist or revolutionary moments are created. According to the experts who study this, the first targets of extremist violent revolutions aren't members of the other side. Before engaging their enemy, they have to purge in-group moderates to create the solidarity they need to take action. This makes total sense. If we're going to engage in a war, I don't want to have to worry about my comrades next to me. Trouble at home needs to be settled first, then you take on the enemy.

Once the extremists succeed at purging in-group moderates, they are ready to take action against you. Due to *ethos* bias, confirmation bias, wishful thinking bias, and other natural impediments to reason, talking sense into this group from the outside is going to be near impossible. I'm watching this happen in real time as some members of the left are trying to cancel other people on the left for being against Hamas. Once you let it get to a point where the moderates have been purged, there is nothing you can do besides put on your Machiavellian hat and defeat them, because they're trying to defeat you. When someone forces you into the jungle, there is no argument or compromise. There is no good faith. There is only victory or defeat.

Let's review where we're at. Purging in-group moderates is step one. This is happening as we speak in the United States on both sides of the aisle. Democrats are canceling each other, and Trump is purging moderate conservatives who aren't loyal to him from the party. Step two is the beginning of violent extremist acts that generate real grievances. These real grievances trigger retaliatory violent acts, which causes the cycle of hatred to begin. This grows faster and faster until we're forced to think like Machiavellians, which we don't want to have to do.

How do we stop this story, and avoid ending up in an ugly,

violent place domestically? The solution is simple. We need to stop purging people from our party. This means moderates need to not purge the extremists, and extremists need to not purge the moderates. For anyone trying to purge you, be stubbornly positive and remain in the group. We need to respect our intraparty differences while recognizing the fundamental truths and objectives we agree on. Decline to be purged. Decline the hostility. Stop this train before it goes too far and becomes unstoppable.

Many moderates will have an inclination to purge extremists from their party. While this is understandable, I don't think this is the best long-term solution. When you "purge" extremists, they don't actually go anywhere, they just aren't welcome. This means they will continue to radicalize and spread their ideas among each other. You'll end up with a cancerous counterculture growing that you have to deal with later. Instead of purging them and leaving them to their own devices, we should bring them in, and embrace them with reason and good faith.

The Honorable Machiavellian

The term "honorable Machiavellian" appears to be an oxymoron. I don't believe it is, based on my definition of Machiavellian. In the jungle, Machiavellianism is a valid, functional worldview. The jungle is a bad place; we don't want to go there. As long as the people we're interacting with are willing to play the civilization game with us, we should play it, and play it honorably. We should never be the ones who ruin the game, and force others into the jungle because we feel it will benefit us. There are few things more sacred than maintaining the civilization game.

However, when interacting with someone, or a group of people, who believe it's advantageous to force us into the jungle, we have to know the rules. Machiavellians are predictable because they play by the rules of the jungle. Sure, they'll try to be crafty like a fox, but you know where they're going. They're going toward what they believe to be their self-interest. They won't be impeded by honesty or any form of morality. When you're pulled into the jungle, you either play by the rules or you get defeated.

As a young liberal, I was against spending a lot of money on the military. However, having incredible military power, in addition to strong alliances, aligns our interests with Machiavellians in the jungle. We want to be so powerful that a Machiavellian knows he will lose if he challenges us. This is an argument a Machiavellian understands. The Machiavellian doesn't care about you. He doesn't care who he hurts. He only cares about himself, and potentially his people. If it's bad for him and his people to harm you, you've successfully achieved peace in the jungle. Peace through strength.

We can't get caught sleeping in the jungle. The jungle is the realest reality. We need to protect ourselves here so we can play the civilization game. We need to understand Machiavellian rules so we can deal with Machiavellian actors. Non-Machiavellian deterrents won't work against a Machiavellian.

Why is human history filled with so many wars? This isn't a question with a singular answer. However, we've already discussed the primary reason; it's highly valuable. Global power politics is like a game of chess, except instead of taking the piece off the board when you capture it, it simply becomes your piece.

Why wouldn't a Machiavellian commandeer his neighbor's home if there were no police to stop him, and he has a superior force? Given that we don't expect our leaders to care much about others, and actively punish them for doing so, the leader who periodically brings in new homes will be much celebrated. The people will give it a cool name like *Manifest Destiny*. Then they will promptly forget it ever belonged to anyone else due to short attention spans and a self-interest bias.

To reiterate, I'm against leaving the civilization game to act like a Machiavellian, but the United States has in the past. We should only turn to the jungle when our opponents are doing so. We need to look out for opponents who are planning to take us to the jungle while appearing to be playing the civilization game.

Being forced into the jungle to act like a Machiavellian is one of the biggest weaknesses of the human condition on earth. When someone forces you into the jungle, you either win or you lose. That means you better win. Even if you want to be honorable, you can get dragged into the mud. Acting like you're still civilized in the mud just means you lose. I'd rather not have to spend over 10% of my budget to stop my neighbors from attacking me. Though if I don't, they're going to attack me because it would be in their Machiavellian interest to do so. Not all of our neighbors would, because not everyone is a Machiavellian. However, leaders are pressured to think that way, so there is likely some Machiavellian who will test you if you show weakness.

Some may think I'm overly pessimistic when I claim that the jungle is the realest reality. Let's explore a hypothetical situation. Suppose a scientist in North Korea invents the first generally intelligent AI program. This program is able to improve itself with the speed of a quantum computer, and within two days it has learned more than humans would have in the next two hundred years.

It invents a new weapon system that can make all North Koreans immune to attack, and allows them to kill as many people as they want anywhere in the world. If North Korea ends up able to kill us and we can't kill them, the civilization game is over. All it would take is a few examples of their power, and we'd fall in line. Either we'd fall in line or we'd fall six feet under. Either way, we lose. We would be effectively at their whims forever unless we could figure out how that technology works to protect ourselves.

I used the North Koreans in this example, but how many other nations or individuals would you trust to have that kind of power? Well, the truth is we kind of already do have the power, we just don't have the defense. With nuclear weapons alone, we would have a good chance at causing human extinction if we were insane enough to try. The good thing is, Machiavellianism can protect us here. Extinction is in no one's Machiavellian interest. However, once the Machiavellian has immunity due to some amazing defense technology, aggression becomes much more attractive. If such a good defense exists, I hope we get it first, or we all get it at the same time.

What happens when someone forces you into the jungle, but they are a fanatical extremist who doesn't fear death? This person is not a Machiavellian; he's not predictable. This person is like Benjamin, the extremist, from chapter 7. The deterrent against a Machiavellian is that we're strong enough to cause you so much harm, it's not in your interest to attack us. Make that Machiavellian argument to Benjamin, and it won't be effective at all. A Machiavellian is a much better enemy than Benjamin is.

State of the Jungle

If we're really in the jungle, what's the state of the jungle right now? Let's start with an overview of the current context. The West, led by the United States, has been the king of the jungle since World War II. Over time, however, China has become a new powerhouse.

China plays the civilization game well, and they prefer to. As China continues to build up its economic and military strength, they become increasingly likely to flex their muscles in a Machiavellian way on the Taiwan issue.

Due to a dependency on Russian energy, the West engaged in willful ignorance with respect to Vladimir Putin's Machiavellianism. We hoped he was playing a civilized game, but we ignored his Machiavellian moves like the annexation of Crimea in 2014. Due to the unprecedented relative global peace among great powers in recent decades, the world underestimated the brutality Putin was willing to commit for Russia's interests.

This triggered a rude awakening that made other countries in the neighborhood, even historically neutral ones, want protection from NATO. They just watched one neighbor, Russia, burn their other neighbor's house down with their family and dog inside. NATO is a group of neighbors that stand together against that kind of thing, but since that particular neighbor wasn't in NATO, Russia knew it could attack without catastrophic consequences. This is not an argument that Ukraine should be in NATO; that would have likely triggered Russian aggression as well. Regardless, Sweden and Finland didn't feel comfortable watching their neighbors burn without having backup, so they moved to join NATO.

The United States is still powerful, but has more threats in the jungle near its own size now. The United States is also sick, suffering internal strife as tribalism weakens its relationships with its allies, and makes it unable to stick to a cohesive strategy over time. There are two keys to the downfall of the United States.

First, its non-Western competitors must stick together and present a united front against the West. Together, they are a great force that represents a more balanced world order than the unipolar

Western-dominated jungle it had been in previous decades. The second key is for them to encourage the United States to retreat into a cave and abandon its allies. To do this, they need to fan the flames of tribalism, and support far-right protectionist politicians. These politicians have already expressed plans to retreat from the world stage, and leave their friends hanging.

Israel is engaged in a non-Machiavellian conflict with religious extremist group Hamas. It's not Machiavellian because Hamas is motivated by religion at least as much as they are by self-interest, if not more. In addition to the physical war, there is a public opinion war taking place. The situation is complex, due to the presence of innocent Palestinians who have real grievances against the Israelis. Hamas wants Israel to kill as many innocent Palestinians as possible. They try to force this to happen by using Palestinians as human shields.

Hamas's goal is to make Israel look as bad as possible. The worse Israel looks, the more support Hamas will receive from neighboring Islamic countries they want to solidify their relationships with and, as importantly, ruin Israel's relationship with. This has the beneficial side effect of fueling tribalism and antisemitism in the United States.

This conflict has caused many of us on the left to get confused, equating Hamas with Palestinians, and blaming Israel for the situation. The worst-case scenario is that Hamas wins the public opinion war, and is able to lure other Muslim nations in the area into attacking Israel. If this happens at scale, it would prompt the West to join in, and who knows where that escalation would end.

I don't mean to dismiss the rest of the world, but it would take too long to cover every country, and I'm not well-informed on all of them. One thing I'd like to mention, however, is why it appears the United States cares about Ukraine so much. Brutal invasions happen in places like Africa and South America, and we don't do much about it. Is the difference due to the skin color of the victims? I don't think so. I think it's due to the perpetrator.

Russia is powerful enough to be a global threat. If we don't make it clear that it's against their interest to take land by force, they would be wise from a Machiavellian perspective to continue to do so. We'd be fools to imagine they are restrained by honor. As such, we have to align Putin's interests with our own, so he knows further violence is bad for both him, and for Russia. Ukraine isn't what's special here, Russia is. The Kremlin is simply too big to fail.

11. Strength Before Weakness

"What is the most important step a man can take?"
— Nohadon

♪ Wild World | Cat Stevens

"Life before death. Strength before weakness. Journey before destination." This is the first ideal of a group called the Knights Radiant, from Brandon Sanderson's *Stormlight Archive*. Sanderson is a much better writer than I am; if you enjoy good stories, I recommend checking out his work. Though Sanderson writes fiction, there is much wisdom to be learned from it. As I said before, literature is art, and art is a portal to other contexts. Experiencing other contexts, even as a spectator, can teach valuable lessons if you're paying attention.

The key driver of political tribalism today isn't policy, but the culture wars. As it relates to raising the next generation, conservatives believe that we on the left are weak and oversensitive. They don't want these characteristics rubbing off on their children. These aren't policy disagreements, but cultural contentions. Though there is certainly a place for sensitivity, our conservative friends care about the future too, and they make some valid points. We have a tendency to write them off as callous, but we should try to understand them, in good faith.

Sticks and Stones

When I was in elementary school, a classmate said something bad about my mom, so I punched him in the face. I was wrong for that. I got in trouble at school, as I should have, and then I had a conversation about it with my parents when I got home. They explained that though it isn't nice to make fun of people's family, it's just words. I had taken a verbal conflict and turned it into a physical one; that meant I was the one in the wrong. They taught me that I should be able to hear people say disrespectful or mean things without resorting to violence, or letting it bother me too much. Perhaps if Will Smith had an experience like mine, the 2022 Oscars would have gone more smoothly.

This chapter is about strength not because we should be macho tough guys. It's about strength because we should be sturdy and resilient. Like my personal example above, conditioning for strength should begin early, during childhood. Childhood should be a training period for adulthood. Adulthood is going to kill you. Not only that, adulthood is going to give you some combination of illness, heartbreaks, loneliness, failures, embarrassment, poverty, physical pain, hopelessness, and more. Life is hard. If we don't prepare our children for it, life will run them over, and it will be our fault.

A common liberal strategy for raising children is to attempt to protect them from the world. To make their childhood a curated bubble where everything is as happy and as great as it can possibly be. There are no losers; everyone gets a participation trophy. It's unacceptable to have to endure any sort of discomfort. If a peer calls him stupid, we have to make sure they are separated so they never have to hear that again. Our hearts are in the right place when we do this, but we're doing our children no favors in the long run.

If your child breaks down when a peer calls him stupid, how is he going to handle it when he hears girls joking about how ugly he is? When the love of his life leaves him? When his dog gets hit by a car, and he watches it suffer until it is put down? Those things hurt far more. Far deeper. Things like that will happen. You can't protect him forever. If your child can't endure discomfort, how do you expect her to focus for the long hours required to have a successful academic career? If you don't discipline your child, how is he going to enjoy life when he's so toxic that the only person who likes him is you? Not even you.

Life is brutal. Instead of living in a bubble afraid of the world, we should teach our children to take control of it, as much as possible. To explore and build callouses from experience. To forge a will of iron such that when they encounter hardships, they aren't destroyed by them. We shouldn't believe in ourselves because no one has said anything mean to us yet. We should believe in ourselves regardless of what anyone says. Confidence from within. Steady, strong, antifragile. These are ideals. We're human, and we all fall short sometimes. Not everyone will be equally resilient, but that's not an excuse to stop trying.

I agree that people should be nice and treat each other with respect. I just know empirically that some people won't do that. You should be able to endure your peers calling you stupid, ugly, fat, stinky, poor, and so on. They shouldn't call you those things, but you should be strong enough to endure it without it ruining your life, or causing depression. Words can cause some people to kill themselves, but hoping that no one ever says anything mean to them is a bad long-term strategy.

It's like living as a balloon, and hoping no one ever bumps into you. The problem isn't that someone bumped into you; the problem is that you're a balloon. I understand this can sound callous, but I have love for the balloon. Because of that love, I don't want it to be a balloon. Protect a balloon for a day, and you've protected it for a day. Teach the balloon to be a stone, and you've protected it for life.

The Fall of Men

Feminists rejoice. Young women are thriving. According to the Pew Research Center, 46% of women between the ages of twenty-five and thirty-four have at least a bachelor's degree. For men in the same age group, it's only 36%. This means, in relative terms, there are about 28% more young women than young men with bachelor's degrees.

Historically, men have been more educated than women, often by large margins. Though the overall rate of young adults with a college education was lower in the 1970s, it was common to have upward of 65% more educated young men than young women. By the 1990s, young women had caught up to young men, and they have generally widened the margin since then to end up where we are today. It's much worse in the Black community; according to the National Center for Education Statistics, during the 2018–19 school year, there were two Black women earning college degrees for every one Black man.

I'm happy that women are doing well, honestly. Women had been held back for a very long time. Now that we have to compete on a more-or-less equal playing field, young women are winning, and winning handily. Though I'm sincerely happy that women are doing well, it creates new social challenges we didn't have to manage in the past. Before we discuss the new challenges we face, I'd like to hypothesize about why young women are doing so much better than young men.

First, a disclaimer. This is a hypothesis; just because it's in a book doesn't make it right. I believe that men are more extreme on average than women. This is why men are overrepresented in the top chess players, in prisons, as business leaders, and so forth. I think more men than women will take one thing in life, and then define their identities around mastering it. Consequently, I think the very best performers in domains men care to compete in will remain male-dominated, potentially forever. As I said before, the only way to have an equivalent number of women among the best chess players may be to stop men from playing, or forcing more girls to dedicate their lives to chess. Neither of which sounds like a good idea.

I don't think we'll end up with 50% female CEOs anytime soon, if ever. However, I do think the average young woman has her act together much better than the average young man. I believe this has always been the case. If I need to rely on a sixteen-year-old to be diligent about a task, follow instructions, and complete it with quality, my money is on the girls over the boys.

If young women have always been more mature and reliable than young men, on average, then why only recently are women surpassing men? The obvious candidates are barriers like discrimination being removed, and a cultural shift in our interpretations of traditional gender roles. Less obvious explanations include better products to manage menstrual cycles, contraception, and a change in the nature of work itself.

When I would speak to my grandfathers about the work they

did, I would hear things like coal mining, steel mills, working the land as a farmer, and tossing heavy bags of salt. If those kinds of careers were how you earned money to take care of a family, men were simply biologically better at them than women. Why would I have my pregnant wife struggle to toss one-hundred-pound bags of salt while I stay home and cook for her? It doesn't make sense. She would likely get fired anyway because she couldn't perform as well as her male coworkers. That type of work was simply better for men.

Fast-forward to today, and the best way to support your family isn't with your muscles, some grit, and work ethic. It's by knowing how to do valuable things that others don't know how to do. In the past, a young man could afford to be a joking fool until age twenty, get his partner pregnant, then decide to "be a man." All he needed to do was use his muscles and show up to work to provide for his family. Simple. Now, if you're a joking fool until you're twenty, working a job with your muscles alone isn't going to do very well for you. If he's wise, the young man will learn a trade, learn to code, or invest in himself in some other way. It's not as easy as it was before to turn physical effort into a respectable living.

Who decides what a respectable living is? Women. When women weren't expected to work, a man who simply chose to have a job was good enough. She was at zero, he was better than that, and there was respect. A good analogy I heard recently is that women like to date men taller than them, but now they're wearing high heels.

Today, the best jobs don't reward muscles; they reward responsibility, knowledge, and diligence. For these criteria, I believe women have the advantage. To the average woman, who can take care of herself, unskilled men are less attractive than they used to be. Instead of settling for men earning less than them, women are looking for men closer to "their level." The problem is the math doesn't add up, and you end up with a bunch of lonely men and women.

Who wins in this environment? Everyone loses except the most successful men. Since women aren't accepting less successful men, that leaves a surplus of women chasing the same few men at the top of the socioeconomic hierarchy. This pattern of women desiring the most successful men isn't new, but it has gotten more extreme as the average woman has become more successful.

If you ask a teacher what the most important things are in life, education will probably rank fairly high. If you ask a personal trainer, he will probably mention fitness fairly quickly. Take this with a grain of salt, but I think an army of lonely, sexually frustrated young men will lead to more tribal extremism. I believe women make us better. It's easy to sit behind a computer, play video games, watch the political outrage machine on social media, and end up as an extreme ideologue. All Aaron Stark needed was a friend to watch a movie and eat pizza with. If he had a good woman at his side, I don't think he would have been close to considering anything so foolish.

The success of women is stressing the social fabric in ways we aren't used to. How do we solve it? Trying to make women less successful is a bad idea. Asking women to settle for more men at the low end of the income distribution probably isn't going to work either. Though a young male extremist may be cured by having a girlfriend, I can't say I blame women for wanting to avoid him. The only answer that I think has a chance to work, is for young men to get better. If men improve themselves, I believe the percentage of "acceptable" men for the average woman can increase.

How do we improve men? First, let's end the negative connotation around masculinity. Specifically, the term *toxic masculinity* comes to mind. While yes, there are some examples of toxic masculinity, masculinity itself isn't toxic. When all masculinity seems bad, boys don't learn how to express it in the right way. They may think that being tough is about violence or aggression. No. Being tough is about discipline, grit, and focus. Confidence and a calculated level of fearlessness. A willingness to bear the burdens others don't want to bear. Endurance and honor. These things make you tough. These things make you competent, reliable, and valuable. Women can be all of these things too.

We liberals have good intentions trying to protect people's feelings, but I believe we're raising boys to be weak men. If a parent treats their son like a balloon who needs to avoid all conflict, stress, and failure, he's going to need to be taken care of. His potential girlfriend isn't likely interested in signing up to be his mother too. His failure in this respect isn't his fault, it's his parents' faults.

Confidence may be what young men need the most. Confidence isn't just useful during the moments you approach a woman and try to fool her into thinking you're an interesting person. That doesn't matter much at all compared to the confidence that becomes a way of life. The confidence to be willing to fail publicly. To believe you can improve yourself. To believe you can accomplish something difficult.

The *Dunning–Kruger* effect describes a pattern whereby the least competent people are about as confident as the most competent people. The more they learn, the more they become aware of the things they don't know, which lowers their confidence. Eventually as they become experts, they get their confidence back again.

Dunning–Kruger

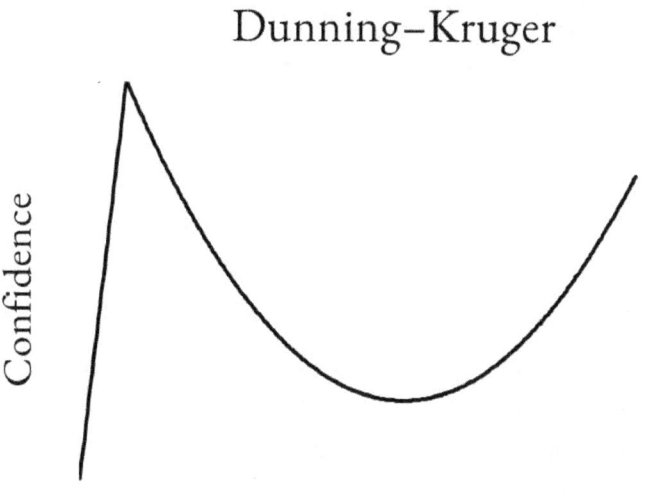

It's a funny phenomenon. Most of us have had experiences with brazenly confident people who had no idea what they were talking about. We can laugh at them, but perhaps there is some value to being confident even when you have no right to be. Confident people usually aren't afraid to take action. You miss 100% of the shots you don't take.

Compound Interest

I remember thinking my uncle was a genius. I was around seven years old, and I was pretty confident in my math skills. Addition, subtraction, multiplication, long division, negative numbers. I thought I knew most of what math had to offer. My uncle was either a sophomore or a junior in high school at the time, and he was doing his math homework. I confidently sauntered up and asked to see it. I was expecting high school math to be hard, but for it to look like this:

10980938.8746 x 898746.37674

I looked at his homework and his math had letters in it:

$9^2/y = 3$

"Oh my God ... These tenth graders are math geniuses," I thought. They were compared to me anyway. I didn't even understand the question because the answer equals 3, obviously. What does it mean to divide 9 small ^{2}s by y? What is the difference between a small ^{2} and a big 2? He still has more years to go until he's a senior. As seniors, are they going to be able to divide 15 small $^{-5}$s by *yoyos*? Are people studying math in college going to be able to divide by whole paragraphs? Do their English classes have a bunch of numbers in them? I gave him his math homework back thoroughly humbled, and grateful I was still in elementary school where math made sense.

Fast-forward to today, and I've done a lot of math compared to the average citizen. I eventually learned Algebra I, Algebra II, geometry, pre-calculus, and calculus before college. I ended up pursuing a master's degree in finance. I had to take lots of accounting, finance, statistics, and economics courses, some of which involved mathematics as advanced as calculus. Of all the math classes I've taken, the hardest was Algebra II.

Why was Algebra II so hard for me, given that I had a much easier time with more advanced mathematics? It wasn't because I had a bad teacher. It wasn't because I was being lazy. It was because

I wasn't prepared. I took Algebra I in a different school district that had a different curriculum. When I started Algebra II in the new school district, they expected me to know things from Algebra I that I had never seen before.

They would say things like, you need to "factor" this out or "foil" it to move on to the next step of solving this problem. I had no idea what "factoring" or "foiling" was. Worst of all, that wasn't even the point of the question; those were just things we were expected to know how to do in order to solve the actual problem. This meant that while my peers could focus on only the new material, I had to spend time catching up to even understand what they were talking about. Only after that, could I learn alongside the rest of the class.

In the beginning of Algebra II, I had lost a bit of confidence in my math skills. Not enough to stop trying, but enough to notice my self-perception change. By the end of Algebra II, I was doing better since I had time to catch up. In my senior year, I ended up getting the highest score possible on the Advanced Placement Calculus test. My confidence was back by then. I realized that none of the math was "hard" necessarily. Seeing letters in math at age seven intimidated me because I didn't know what they were. Being asked to "foil" confused me because I didn't know what it meant. Once I caught up, none of those topics were intimidating anymore.

I then thought about the kids who struggled with their times tables back in elementary school. Perhaps they just didn't have a solid foundation of addition before getting tossed into multiplication. Then after struggling with multiplication, they may have lost confidence and concluded that math wasn't for them. Eventually they would catch up and learn basic multiplication, but they didn't try very hard. Though they had caught up with multiplication, they were still behind on whatever was being taught at the time, like logarithms.

If you ask them today, they may say multiplication and exponents are "easy" compared to the last math they had to do. Though it wasn't easy for them when they first tried it. The pattern I noticed was that all math was "easy" once you knew it, and seemed like hieroglyphics before you learned it. The idea that someone feels like they're "not good at math" because of a chain of events that started with multiplication saddens me. It's human nature to not like things we're not good at. We weren't prepared, so we didn't do well. We didn't do well, so we didn't like it. We didn't like it, so we gave up. Then we decided we must not be one of the smart people, and lost confidence to ever try again.

This is a real cycle where people underestimate themselves into a self-fulfilling prophecy. If you think you can do something, you may be right. If you think you can't do something, you're almost certainly right. I think people overvalue intelligence, and undervalue the cumulative benefits of making good decisions over time.

Suppose I challenged the average American, Nate, to read two hours per day about our solar system for five days in a row. Nate is given a book with everything noteworthy to learn about our solar system. He will learn how many planets there are, and how close they are to the sun. He'll learn about each planet's atmosphere, moons, and cores. About where the asteroids and comets are, the history of Pluto, and so on. Two hours is a long time to focus on something; you can learn a lot in two focused hours. Five days isn't very long in relation to our lives.

At the end of this five-day period, I expect that Nate would know more than probably 98% of people about our solar system. If you can be more knowledgeable than 98% of the population on a subject with just five days of effort, what would four years of effort look like? Imagine Diego is smarter than Nate such that he can learn twice as efficiently, but he only reads one night. At the end of five days, Nate has still more than doubled Diego.

There are gargantuan differences in how people spend their time. Differences in how we spend our time are far greater than differences in our intelligence levels. It's just invisible, so it's difficult for us to recognize. Most of us assume fairness, but it's an illusion. You may see that Ivan has a C in math, and Pete has an A in math, then conclude that Pete is naturally better at math. It's possible, but there are too many unknown variables to draw any conclusions.

Success in a given area is often like climbing a mountain. Some people are faster climbers than others, but even slow climbers can be found at the tops of mountains if they've been climbing consistently. Given the vast differences in how long we've been climbing, you can't tell how fast a climber is based on their position on the mountain.

It's common for people to complain about their position, despite the fact that they haven't spent much effort climbing. Many of the people at the top have been climbing consistently for years. To get where they are, it's a good idea to do what they do. There are sometimes shortcuts because the universe isn't fair, but those are the exceptions to the rule.

It's easy to fall into the trap of thinking you're a bad climber because you're currently low on the mountain. Choosing to climb a different mountain is fine, but when you stop climbing altogether, you're in trouble. The most important step is always the next one. I'd like to end with a personal story to showcase the value of making good decisions over time. Compound interest not of money, but of choices.

It was my senior year in college, and I was in my fifth accounting class. The professor was teaching us how to account for a new scenario we hadn't seen before. After she described the scenario, I formed a hypothesis about how it should be handled based on the accounting principles I knew.

My hypothesis was right. It was a new concept, and I could have correctly solved problems about it using my familiarity with accounting alone as a guide. Many of my classmates sat through the class, were told how to solve it, took notes about it, went home and read about it, tried it as a homework problem, and still ended up getting it wrong.

From an outside perspective, people often jump to the conclusion that I'm just smarter than they are. I don't. I know how they study because I've had conversations with them about it. I know how I study obviously, and if I weren't leagues ahead of them, there would be something wrong with me. This happened in our fifth accounting class. Let's go back to the first week of Accounting 101.

The first assignment was to answer all the even-numbered questions from the first chapter of the book. What did my peers do? They read the questions first, then skimmed the chapter to find the answers. It probably took them ten minutes. What did I do? I read the full chapter at a conversational pace, including examples, and the little stories in the margins. I didn't just read it; I actively took notes in my own words. After I read it once, I rarely needed to look at the chapter again; I would just study from my notes.

Reading and taking detailed notes would take me about an hour, maybe more. Then answering the questions was fast, only taking me a few minutes. They *found* the answers. I *knew* the answers. Not because I was smarter; because I made the decision to study how I studied. They could have made the same decision.

On that first homework assignment, almost all of us got a ten out of ten on it. It wasn't hard. The return on investment for my extra hour spent wasn't immediately clear. But fast-forward four accounting classes later, and is it any surprise that I'm much better than they are at accounting? They see that I can get it right before being taught it. They end up getting it wrong after being taught it, and after hours spent studying. What they don't see, are the fifty to one hundred hours I've already spent more than they have on accounting. How could I not be noticeably better after all of that extra effort? Moreover, staying ahead is more efficient than trying to play catch-up, like I had to do while I was struggling in Algebra II.

You don't have to be naturally fit to run a marathon. You don't have to be naturally "smart" to graduate from college. You don't even have to be smart to make smart decisions. You don't need to be special to have confidence in yourself. Successful people are far more like the rest of us than they are different. If you have discipline, and make good decisions over time, eventually your next step may place you on top of the mountain. Such is the power of compound interest.

Tribalism is a large mountain to climb. We can't scale it overnight. We can, however, take the first step, and then the next one. We can bring a little light with us going forward. We can choose peace every now and then, instead of responding to hostility in kind. We can attempt to understand our friends from across the aisle. We can release some positive butterflies into the world. We may not see the return on our investment immediately. However, neither did Aaron Stark's friend.

12. Finding Us

"The universe is in us. When I reflect on that fact ... I feel big, because my atoms came from those stars."
– Dr. Neil DeGrasse Tyson

♪ Shepherd of Fire | Avenged Sevenfold

I'm writing this book because I'm concerned about the future. About the consequences of tribalism running rampant as technology advances. Artificial intelligence, fusion energy, robotics, scientifically refined social media algorithms, nuclear proliferation, and so on. Some are good, some are bad, and some are both. All are powerful; power can be used both constructively and destructively. These are just the things I foresee impacting us in the next couple of decades. The plan, hopefully, is to be around much longer than that.

It's common for humanity to have periods of hundreds, sometimes thousands of years with very little significant technological change. Recent history is an exception. The Industrial Revolution of the eighteenth and nineteenth centuries transformed the global economy through mass-production manufacturing. Shortly after began the Information Age, where computers and the Internet created entire industries that didn't exist before. We're arguably near the end of the Information Age, approaching a new era of artificial intelligence.

Everyone alive today, and everyone we've known lived either during the Industrial Revolution or the Information Age. This whirlwind of technological advancement is something we're used to, but it isn't normal in the context of human history. These technologies have lifted many people around the world out of poverty. Daily life is much easier now than it used to be due to things like lights, plumbing, automobiles, refrigerators, the Internet, and cell phones.

Roughly coinciding with the Industrial Revolution, we had the Enlightenment. As we transformed our industries with technology like the steam engine, we transformed ourselves with a cultural movement valuing reason and human rights. As civilization became more advanced technologically, it simultaneously became more advanced civilly. I doubt the timing of the Enlightenment to align with the Industrial Revolution was intentional. Nonetheless, improving ourselves as we improve our technology is a pattern we should perpetuate.

To responsibly manage the power bestowed on us by technology, we need to become better people like we did during the Enlightenment. Evolution can't keep up with technology, but culture can. Culture is powerful, and can change quickly. Unfortunately, cultural changes aren't always for the better.

Tribalism is precisely what we don't need defining modern culture as we begin to flex our muscles as a species. I'm being optimistic thinking of the current moment as still being in *Homo sapiens'* adolescence. The current position of the doomsday clock suggests otherwise. The good news is the only thing that can defeat us, besides Mother Nature, is them. Who are they? Us. This book is a warning and a prescription. Take tribalism seriously. To defeat it, we need to attempt to understand each other, in good faith.

The Ultimate Context

The majority of this book is about political conflict between the left and the right, but this is just one specific manifestation of tribalism. We could move to a smaller context and examine tribalism within political parties. At the intraparty level, you have discord between people closer to the center, and people further from it. We could move to a broader context and discuss tribal conflicts between nations or alliances. We could change perspectives and examine tribalism based on ethnicity, which cuts across national identities. Populism could be described as tribalism based on economic class.

What do all of these manifestations of tribalism have in common? A solution. Attempt to understand each other, in good faith. By "good faith," I mean sincere positivity. Tribalism between political parties is highly visible. It's easy to understand. It's something many of us directly participate in. For those reasons, it's a good manifestation to focus on first. However, since the cure for tribalism is the same for all manifestations of it, there is no reason to limit good faith understanding to conversations about Democrats and Republicans. Furthermore, just because political party-based tribalism is the easiest to understand, doesn't mean it's the most important. The question of importance brings us to the concept of the holy.

I first heard about this version of "the holy" during my undergraduate course Problems in Philosophy. My professor defined "the holy" as the ultimate context. He broke it down like this. We're currently in this classroom, which is in the context of the building. The building is in the context of the university, which is in the context of the city of New Orleans. New Orleans is in the context of the State of Louisiana, which is in the context of the United States. The

United States is in the context of North America, which is in the context of the earth. The earth is in the context of our solar system, which is in the context of the Milky Way galaxy. Continue this process until you get to a context that has no greater enveloping context. Whatever that ultimate context is, he called "the holy."

This was one of the conversations we had disagreements about. I appreciated the idea of examining the ultimate context, but I didn't think the word "holy" had anything to do with it. I argued that it unnecessarily added a religious element to the conversation. It was during a back-and-forth on this topic that my professor criticized me for looking at opposing ideas as concepts to be shot down, instead of as opportunities to improve my perspective. I'm still not a fan of the term "holy," but contexts are a core element of this book, and we're about to explore the ultimate context of tribalism. Moreover, his criticism of me was both valid and valuable, so out of respect for that, I'll continue to use the term.

I asked this question rhetorically in chapter 4, but what is the holy, the ultimate context, as it relates to tribalism? As we discussed above, tribalism comes in a myriad of flavors. There is tribalism based on politics, ethnicity, social class, religion, etc. Each of those broad flavors of tribalism can be broken down into different contextual levels. For example, tribalism between different sects of the same faith is a smaller context than tribalism between entirely different faiths. When you examine the highest contexts of each flavor of tribalism and try to fit them together, it all boils down to conflict between groups of people. This means that addressing tribalism in the ultimate context is essentially a quest for peace.

The topic of peace brings us to the Fermi paradox. Dr. Enrico Fermi was something of a child prodigy who grew to become a Nobel laureate in physics. Fermi worked with Robert Oppenheimer as an associate director in the Manhattan Project. In the Standard Model of particle physics, there is a group of subatomic particles called "fermions" that was named after him.

We've established that Fermi was an accomplished physicist, now let's explore his paradox. It all boils down to a single question: "Where is everybody?" This was the question Fermi asked at lunch during a conversation with friends about extraterrestrial life. Simply put, the odds seem very high that there would be intelligent alien life in our galaxy, yet we don't see any evidence of it. That's the paradox in a nutshell, but let's break down how Fermi arrived at his conclusion.

Thinking like a scientist, we need to zoom out and analyze at the scale of the universe, as opposed to the scale of a human life. Individual humans will live one hundred years, if we're lucky. Our species has been on earth approximately three hundred thousand years. Even this amount of time pales in comparison to the age of the Milky Way galaxy which, according to our best estimates, is over ten billion years old.

The ingredients for life as we know it are quite simple. You need a star, temperatures that allow water to remain in a liquid state, water, carbon, and nitrogen. Astrophysicist Dr. Neil DeGrasse Tyson explained quite clearly how common the ingredients of life are in the universe.

"The four most common chemically active elements in the universe—hydrogen, oxygen, carbon, and nitrogen—are the four most common elements of life on Earth. We are not simply in the universe. The universe is in us."

In the Milky Way galaxy alone, there are a few hundred billion stars. Some fraction of them will have planets. Some fraction of those planets will have temperatures in ranges where water can be liquid. Some fraction of those will have water, carbon, and nitrogen, which, as Dr. Tyson explained, are quite common. Then the only thing you need is time, and we have over ten billion years of that. Even if only a fraction of 1% of star systems have all of the ingredients necessary for life, given that there are hundreds of billions of star systems, you'd expect to see a lot of life in our galaxy.

Once we've established the very high statistical likelihood of alien life, it's not a difficult leap to assume that some fraction of the planets with life may eventually develop intelligence, as we have. If intelligence lasts any significant amount of time at the scale of the galaxy, we'd expect them to be able to accomplish great things. We didn't do much for three hundred thousand years, but just in the last five hundred years our technological capabilities have skyrocketed. We went from no electricity to the Internet, nuclear weapons, and artificial intelligence. What would a civilization with our intelligence be able to accomplish if it lasted merely another three hundred thousand years? This is practically no time at all to the universe; it would just be an intelligent species twice as old as we are.

With hundreds of billions of star systems, and over ten billion years of time, we'd expect some intelligent civilizations to be out and about. Even if our intelligent friends' spaceships only move at a small fraction of the speed of light, given the age of the galaxy, that's still plenty of time for them to have explored and left some evidence of their activity. This brings us back to Fermi's question, "Where is everybody?"

There are a few possible answers to this question that are quite simple. Perhaps the galaxy is actually teeming with intelligent life, but there is relatively little activity in our neck of the woods. Just because you don't see any tigers when you look out the window, doesn't mean there aren't any tigers in the world. Another possibility is that there are signals from intelligent life, we just haven't developed the technology necessary to detect them yet.

The answer I'm concerned about is a phenomenon called "the Great Filter." Renowned theoretical physicist Dr. Stephen Hawking explored this very concern in the last book he wrote before passing away, *Brief Answers to the Big Questions*. Dr. Hawking wrote, "It is not even clear that intelligence has any long-term survival value." Thinking at the scale of the layperson, this seems preposterous. Of course intelligence is good for survival; humans are the most powerful species on earth. If we instead think like a scientist, we realize that life has been on earth in some form for about 3.5 billion years. Early on it wasn't complex animal life, but it was life. Life has proven itself to be fairly stable and long-lasting without intelligence. Our measly three hundred thousand years isn't nearly enough time to determine whether or not human-level intelligence is beneficial for a species' survival in the long run.

As it relates to the Great Filter, Hawking had the following remarks. "A third possibility is that there is a reasonable probability for life to form and to evolve into intelligent beings, but the system becomes unstable and the intelligent life destroys itself. This would be a very pessimistic conclusion and I very much hope it isn't true." Hawking was primarily concerned about three risks—nuclear war, climate change, and artificial intelligence. In the following excerpt, he discusses two of them, along with his responsibility as a scientist to warn the public:

> "As scientists, we understand the dangers of nuclear weapons, and their devastating effects, and we are learning how human activities and technologies are affecting climate systems in ways that may forever change life on earth. As

citizens of the world, we have a duty to share that knowledge, and to alert the public to the unnecessary risks that we live with every day. We foresee great peril if governments and societies do not take action now, to render nuclear weapons obsolete and to prevent further climate change."

Scientists discover and invent technologies that give us great power. If we can efficiently use fusion energy, we will have the power of miniature suns at our fingertips. Scientists give us this power, and then whoever wins the popularity contest of politics wields it. It's the scientists' job to warn us. It's our job to heed their warnings.

If the Great Filter is a real phenomenon, and intelligence isn't compatible with long-term survival, then the time when the filtering happens is right now. We didn't have the power to get filtered three hundred years ago. We're among the first generations that have the responsibility to avoid being filtered. If we continue to behave as we've been behaving, we're not going to make it, it's filtering time. If we do plan to survive, which I hope we can agree is a good plan, it's not going to be possible with tribalism running amok, and people inventing group-based reasons to kill each other. If we plan to be here in the long run, we'll need to get our act together. We might as well start now.

Personally, I don't believe the Great Filter is inevitable. I believe that intelligence can be compatible with long-term survival. If it strictly isn't, then we're doomed anyway. We may as well behave as if it is, since it's our only chance. What I'm concerned about is the possibility that we're in a negative Goldilocks zone. A situation where we're intelligent enough to gain the power to destroy civilization, yet not intelligent enough to figure out how to refrain from doing so.

The test for whether or not we'll soon be filtered isn't one of mathematics. It's not a test of science or statistics. You won't find the answers on the SAT. It's a test of the ultimate context of tribalism. A test of the holy. A test of peace.

Holy Stardust

How are we supposed to pass a test of peace when we have Machiavellians lurking around every corner? Not easily. Hence the barren night sky and the Fermi paradox. The challenge is made more difficult due to the fact that we don't get to pass the test once and then rest on our laurels. We have to continue passing the test on an ongoing basis. Fail once, and the consequences may be catastrophic. In the fall of 2022, President Biden warned of possible "Armageddon" as a consequence of escalation in Vladimir Putin's invasion of Ukraine.

In order to understand why it's so difficult to attain peace when dealing with Machiavellians, we'll turn to game theory. Game theory is essentially an analysis of behavior in a given scenario, called a "game." In game theory, we assume that each player in the game is rational and self-interested, just like a Machiavellian.

Let's go back in time to the beginning of COVID-19. Hank hears a rumor that there may soon be a shortage of toilet paper. For reasons he doesn't understand, some of his peers have already begun panic-buying the product, but it's not widespread yet. Hank, like practically everyone else, wouldn't enjoy running out of toilet paper. Hank and the public have the same decision to make. Should they panic-buy large quantities of toilet paper, or purchase their usual quantity?

If Hank chooses to purchase a normal quantity of toilet paper, and the vast majority of his peers choose to do the same, everyone will have clean behinds. This is the best-case scenario for society. If Hank purchases a normal quantity, and enough of his peers begin panic buying, he'll have some creative problem-solving to do in the bathroom. If Hank were a Machiavellian, he'd think to himself, "I'm not going to be one of the suckers without toilet paper." Then he would choose the only option that guarantees winning this game; he'd panic-buy toilet paper, and shallowly wish good luck upon everyone else.

Perhaps the most popular scenario in game theory is called the prisoner's dilemma. We'll discuss a variant of it with Hank as one of the players. In this scenario, Hank is a low-ranking member of a large criminal drug organization. Hank was involved in a crime with three other people when all four of them were arrested by the police.

Based on the evidence the police have, they can send Hank and his coconspirators to prison for two years each. However, each of them knows high-ranking leaders of the criminal organization. If these leaders were to fall, the organization would go down with them. The police would much rather bring down the entire criminal enterprise than punish a few foot soldiers. So, each of them is offered a deal by law enforcement. Give them the information they need to bring down the organization, and you can go free with no prison time. If one of your three peers accepts this deal before you do, you'll go to prison for ten years. If no one accepts the deal, the four go to prison for two years, and the criminal operation continues in good health.

What does Hank do? If Hank is a Machiavellian, he doesn't want to end up wasting ten years of his life because someone else worked with the police first. Besides, Hank doesn't trust his "coworkers," they're criminals. The Machiavellian choice is clearly to work with the police and go home scot-free.

If you're a responsible leader of a criminal enterprise, you can't afford to let your entire business get destroyed every time a low-ranking member gets caught by the police. The Machiavellian tendency to work with the police after getting caught is incredibly selfish. If Hank and his coconspirators had honor, they could just serve two years each, and the organization would continue to thrive. Instead, in order to avoid prison time for themselves, they condemn tens of other people in the organization to over a decade in prison, destroying an operation worth millions of dollars.

Responsible criminal leaders understand the Machiavellian tendency for people to work with the police after being caught. To reduce risk, criminal leaders often decide to add some extra incentives to the Machiavellian's decision calculus. This is where the saying "Snitches get stitches" comes from. Suppose the criminal organization has a policy such that if one of its members works with the police, they will be tracked down and assassinated. Given that the threat is credible and there is a history of enforcement, working with the police may no longer be the most attractive Machiavellian option.

Suppose the policy isn't just assassination of the snitch, but also the assassination of their known family members. That's an even more persuasive policy. If I were to work in a criminal organization, I'd feel safer with a strong anti-snitching program. It makes the entire organization more stable. Even better, add a carrot with the stick. Offer "insurance" by providing support to the families of anyone who gets sent to prison while doing business for the organization.

We're examining the perspective of criminal leaders because

they are tasked with protecting the longevity of an organization made up of Machiavellian actors who have incentives to destroy it. They need to align each individual's Machiavellian interest with the interest of the organization as a whole. If the leader fails in this endeavor, the entire organization is going to take a major blow every time a low-ranking member gets handcuffed. That criminal enterprise would soon be filtered.

Aligning Machiavellian interests as a leader in a criminal enterprise is much easier than aligning Machiavellian interests in geopolitics. First of all, the "leader" in the criminal enterprise has authority. There is no authority in geopolitics; each nation is a peer. We can't just declare policies and expect everyone else to enforce them. In a criminal enterprise, the leader can use both the carrot and the stick as tools to align interests. In geopolitics, using too much of the stick is going to create the very situation you're trying to avoid. As it relates to the carrot, it's difficult to find carrots that are more attractive than the Machiavellian benefits of conflict.

So, does this mean we're doomed? Perhaps. The picture is grim, but there is one silver lining that I can see. If the criminal leader credibly promises to assassinate the snitch, that's a strong incentive against working with the police. If the leader also credibly promises to assassinate the snitch's family, that's a stronger incentive. This means that the Machiavellian isn't just self-interested. That's an oversimplification. The Machiavellian is "us-interested." The question is, who is included in "us"?

If "us" only includes the Machiavellian himself, then us-interest is equal to self-interest. However, as "us" grows to include more people, it becomes increasingly different from self-interest, and our previous analysis of the game becomes less valid. Changing the players changes the game.

The more people who are included in "us," the more stable the system becomes. If "us" includes the entire criminal organization, then you don't need carrots or sticks. Everyone would still be a Machiavellian, but they would all act in the Machiavellian interest of the organization. It would become a game with a single player, the organization. This level of interest alignment is a goal that is shared by large corporations. The difference is that employees of corporations don't tend to have interactions with police that provide a strong incentive to destroy the company.

How large can "us" feasibly be, given human nature? Capitalism works quite well, and it assumes individuals are self-interested. Historically, experiments implementing extreme collectivism haven't worked out very well. It's practically impossible for "us" to include the entire organization for everyone in the organization. Again, are we doomed? Based on game theory and the Fermi paradox, most likely, but not necessarily. We're still exploring the silver lining.

In order to avoid being filtered, the enterprise must continue operations. This means that every key person in the organization who has the power to bring it down, needs to have an "us" that includes the entire organization. This way even if low-ranking members work with the police, they will only be able to go up the chain so far. Eventually, they would hit a wall with someone who is unwilling to give them information that would deal a critical blow to the enterprise.

This means that your low-ranking members shouldn't have the power to bring the organization down. Moreover, the organization should seek to minimize the number of individuals who singlehandedly have the ability to critically injure it. A system with elements of a democracy can accomplish this goal. This way, even when you inevitably have some purely self-interested Machiavellian officers, they at least have to act like they care about the organization. More importantly, one bad apple can't ruin the bunch.

As human society is constructed today, as soon as an extremist tyrant gets his hands on a powerful nuclear arsenal, that one individual can threaten the existence of many species on earth, including our own. This is not a stable system in the long run. Geopolitically, the most attainable stable system doesn't require the entire world to have a broad "us." We just need the countries that are powerful enough to cause us to get filtered to have a broad "us."

The above is far from easy. However, key-player peace is much more achievable than total world peace. Even considering only key players, we're still talking about a lot of countries and a lot of people. Can "us" really be that big? Intuitively, many people will think the answer is no. They may be right, but I'm not certain.

You wouldn't expect any nation to hit themselves with a devastating attack. This means that "us" can be as broad as a nation. How big can a nation be? The largest nation by landmass is Russia, at over sixteen million square kilometers. China and India are by far the largest nations by population, with over 1.4 billion people each. In comparison, the United States has only three hundred million people, and nine million square kilometers of land.

So, we know that "us" can be as large as 1.4 billion people, or sixteen million square kilometers. I don't see any clear reason "us" couldn't become significantly larger on either metric. To get all of the key players on board, I estimate that we'd need to create an "us" that is about three times as broad as the largest we've created so far. This would be no walk in the park, but what other options do we have if we plan to avoid being filtered?

Personally, I think the challenge will not be one of geography or of population, but of cultural cohesion. The United States is a very diverse country, but we're called the "melting pot" for a reason. We're supposed to melt and become one, as Americans. Spreading a positive culture around the world makes it easier to have the cohesion necessary to expand "us." This has already happened before with the spread of Enlightenment values and capitalism around the world. They aren't everywhere, but they are common enough to provide a shared foundation for most modern nations.

In chapter 10, "Welcome to the Jungle," I compared war to chess. It's similar, but instead of taking pieces you capture off the board, they become your pieces instead. If a Machiavellian can invade a country and then make it their own, that's an enormous incentive for initiating a war. A smart Machiavellian will conjure up a pretext of course, but the real reason is all of the benefits that come along with stealing an entire country.

I'm bringing up the Machiavellian incentives for war again because there are ways to reduce the attractiveness of this incentive. The more interconnected two nations' economies are, the less likely they are to have conflicts. This is a lesser-appreciated benefit of the European Union (EU). The fact that EU nations share a currency and central bank makes it less attractive for member nations to attack each other. If both parties were to stay in the EU, neither would singlehandedly have the power to manipulate the monetary policy of the euro for their benefit.

A nation doesn't have to be part of a formal institution like the EU for peer nations to impose economic disincentives for Machiavellian aggression. The Machiavellian wants to steal the country because countries are worth a lot of money, in addition to their strategic value. However, if stealing that country causes the Machiavellian to lose enough customers for their core products, it may not be worth it. Whether it's worth it or not depends on how many customers they lose, and for how long the customers commit to avoiding their products.

Put simply, in the Machiavellian's short-term interest, aggression often is a good move, if you can win. In the long term, aggression is only worth it if the benefit gained is greater than the cost imposed on you by your peers. This means that even third parties have an important role to play in managing the Machiavellian interest of powerful actors. We need to make it clear that aggression will not work out favorably for a Machiavellian in the long run, especially for key players. However, we can't hold grudges indefinitely, lest an eye for an eye end up making the whole world blind. The cost imposed should be strong enough to clearly give the Machiavellian regret for having made the move, but not be so long-lasting as to sentence us to perpetual conflict.

It's practically impossible to rid the world of Machiavellian behavior. It's ingrained in human nature so deeply that even a tool as powerful as culture may not be able to dispose of it. We'll never be rid of Machiavellians, but we can align interests with them. Aligning interests, in combination with building good faith relationships can allow us to potentially end up being part of the same "us." A Machiavellian isn't dangerous when you're a bona fide member of her "us."

I can understand someone feeling like this conversation is a bit pie-in-the-sky. Passing a test of peace at the scale of humanity? Worrying about the Fermi paradox and being filtered? People are worried about the cost of housing and health care, things that impact our daily lives. To this I respond, you're right, but we need to be able to walk and chew gum at the same time.

Solving a problem at the scale of the Fermi paradox is like creating a new Grand Canyon. We're not going to be able to do it with a bulldozer by the end of the year. We can, however, use running water to form the canyon slowly over time. The executable goal isn't to defy the Fermi paradox. It's to make today better than yesterday. It is over time, with the compound interest of positive butterflies that we'll be able to impact the holy.

Speaking of impacting the holy, we've come full circle back to the late Carl Sagan. Dr. Sagan was a spiritual scientist in pursuit of peace. He helped keep the Cold War in the refrigerator. He worked to establish a relationship of cooperation, not competition, between the United States and the Soviet Union. He was an American. A human. An intelligent animal. He was stardust. Not just any stardust. Stardust that found "us."

To most people, he's just a man. A scientist. I prefer to think of him as holy stardust. What kind of stardust are you?

Index

A

Abortion, 2, 49, 60, 138
Adulthood, 218
Americantribe, 48, 123
An Inconvenient Truth, 41, 53
Anthony, Oliver, 163
Antisemitism, 215
Aristotle, 33, 36
Armstrong, Louis, 33, 85
Artificial intelligence, 233, 238–239
Asians, 135–136
Asylum, 183–186, 189
Autism, 160

B

Baptists, 11
Barbarism, 208
Bin Laden, Osama, 155
Black community, 135, 151, 159, 220
Black crime, 136
Black man, 20, 51, 220
Black people, 65, 78, 80–82, 94, 102, 133–135, 137, 139, 151, 159–160, 165
Black transpeople, 192
Black tribe, 47
Blundering foreign policy, 4
Boiled Frog Problems, 51
Border control, 49

Breach of fiduciary duty, 200–201
Brutal invasions, 216
Buddhism, 123
Bush, George W., 182, 188
Business regulations, 49
Butterfly effect, 5–6, 10, 18, 20–21

C

Capitalism, 40–41, 190–191, 195, 245, 247
Catholics, 11, 152
Cheney, Liz, 58–59
Childhood, 1, 6, 218
China, 28, 31, 72, 193, 213–214, 246
Christian tribe, 47
Christianity, 11, 123, 127
Cisgender White males, 192
Climate change, 5, 41, 52–53, 68, 71, 73, 118–119, 189, 193, 239–240
Clinton, Bill, 72, 185
Coefficient of correlation, 105
Coefficient of determination, 105, 137
Cold War, 16, 249
Confidence, 6, 33, 59–60, 66, 70, 76, 83, 202, 205, 219, 224, 227–228, 231

Consensus, 73–74, 76

Corruption, 7, 30, 108, 118, 145, 166

COVID-19, 70, 75, 241

Crime, 7, 15, 109, 116, 118, 133–137, 139, 165, 181, 202–203, 242

Criminals, 72, 101, 135, 137, 140, 166, 169, 184, 202–203, 205, 243

Critical race theory, 61–62

Crow, Jim, 65, 80

Cuban, Mark, 139

Cultural changes, 109, 234

Culture war, 78, 109, 174, 217

D

Dark environments, 17

Deif, Mohammed, 208

Democrats, 11, 27, 46, 49, 57–58, 62–63, 174, 181–182, 184–185, 202, 209, 235

Deportation, 181–182

Deporter in chief, 181

DeSantis, Ron, 26, 163, 181

Difficulty, 7–8
  Cognitive, 8–9
  Competitive, 8–9
  Will, 3–5, 7–10

Diplomatic relationships, 108

Disagreements, 58, 78–79, 122, 146–147, 149

Factual, 149

Fundamental, 149

Religious, 122, 151

Discrimination, 7, 80, 161, 169, 221

Disease resistance, 109

Disgust, 80, 133, 170

Divided We Fall, 27, 207

Dunning-Kruger effect, 224

E

Economic system, 41, 108

Education systems, 108

Einstein, Albert, 75, 111

Electoral college, 49, 62, 64

Embarrassment, 46, 218

Empiricism, 107, 109, 111, 114, 123

Environmental policy, 49

Ethnic diversity, 109

Ethos, 33–37, 40, 45, 61, 94, 133, 139, 209

European Union (EU), 247

Extremism, 83, 152, 190, 207, 223

F

factors, 104

Fear, 58–59, 61–62, 90, 92, 133, 137–138, 151, 158, 183–184, 193, 202, 207, 213

Female tribe, 48

Feminists, 220

Fermi, Enrico, 236

Fermi paradox, 236, 241, 245, 248–249
Fiduciary duty, 199–201
Fiscal policy, 5, 49
Foreign policy, 4, 28, 49, 78, 190, 204, 206
French, David, 207, 209
Fusion energy, 233, 240

G

GDP, 105–106, 188
Gendron, Payton, 150, 173
Generalizing the individual, 138–139
Global power politics, 30, 211
Good faith, 2–4, 6, 8–12, 14, 16–22, 88, 90–92, 214, 216–218, 240, 242
Goodness, 120, 166, 196–199
Gorbachev, Mikhail, 16
Gore, Al, 41, 52, 188
GPA, 104
Great Replacement theory, 173
Gun regulations, 49

H

Hamas, 193, 208–209, 215
Heinrichs, Jay, 33
Heterosexuals, 116
Hinduism, 123
Hispanics, 14, 163
Hollis, Rasaan, 97
Homosapiens, 15, 97–98, 100, 126, 155, 234

Homosexuals, 116, 127
Honor, 20, 58, 64, 98, 142, 174, 196–198, 216, 224, 243
Honorable Machiavellian, 210
Hopelessness, 100, 218
Housing, 12, 189, 248
Human history, 68, 124, 126–127, 211, 234
Human memory, 123
Human nature, 7, 13, 115, 125, 138, 195, 228, 245, 248
Human tribe, 47

I

Immigration, 5, 49, 70, 108, 133, 181, 185
Immigration policy, 108
Individual rights, 108
Intellectual humility, 38, 40, 69
Iran, 193
Iron Knee High School's math team, 145–146
Islam, 123–124, 152
Israel, 30, 193, 204–205, 208, 215
Israeli-Palestinian conflict, 208

J

Jehovah's Witnesses, 124
Jewish, 97, 150–151, 173, 183
Jewish people, 97, 150–151, 183
Jordan, Michael, 13
Judaism, 123

K

Kim Jong Un, 155
Kinzinger, Adam, 58
Kremlin, 216

L

Legal system, 82, 108, 118, 120, 179, 181, 184–186
Lennon, John, 193
LGBTQIA, 49
Logos, 33–37, 46, 51, 94, 133, 138–139

M

Machiavelli, Niccolò, 195
Machiavellianism, 195–196, 210, 213–214
Maher, Bill, 62
Male tribe, 48
Manifest Destiny, 212
Martin Luther King Jr., 13, 17, 65
Math problems, 140, 187
McConnell, Mitch, 62, 64
Melting pot, 247
Mexican migrants, 181
Middle management, 43–46
Mighty Convenience, 40
Migrants, 179, 181, 184, 189
Military strength, 108, 155, 214
Mithraism, 123
Monetary policy, 49, 247
Monotheistic religions, 123
Mormonism, 123–124
Multivariate societal contexts, 102

Mushaddeq, Ahmad, 124
Muslim tribe, 47
Mysterious ways, 126

N

NATO, 28, 193, 204–205, 214
Nazi Germany, 98, 122, 183, 205
Nazis, 183–184
Negative Contexts, 88, 94–95
Neighbors, 108, 190, 212, 214
Netanyahu, Benjamin, 208
Nietzsche, Friedrich, 179
Nohadon, 217
Non-exclusionary, 119
Non-Machiavellian, 211, 215
Non-rivalrous, 119
Nostalgia, 133
Nuclear proliferation, 16, 233

O

Obama, Barack Hussein, 26
Open-mindedness, 9, 142
Oppenheimer, Robert, 236
Orthopraxis, 3
Owens, Candace, 29
Owned slaves, 98

P

Palestinians, 208, 215
Pathos, 33–34, 52, 61–62, 66, 94, 133
Patriarchy, 48
Physical pain, 218
Political issues, 49, 107, 143

Polytheistic religions, 123
Populism, 163, 235
Positive ethos, 37
Potter, Harry, 18
poverty, 22, 87, 165, 218, 234
pro-Palestinian, 208
Psychopaths, 198
Public goods, 119
Purification, 58, 60
The Pursuit of Happiness, 87
Putin, Vladimir, 31, 58, 154–155, 214, 241

R

Racism, 94, 133, 160, 165
Rationalism, 107, 109, 111
Real confidence, 33
Real conservatism, 58
Religion, 15, 91, 97–98, 108–109, 122–128, 151–155, 215, 236
Religious violence, 152
Republican in Name Only (RINO), 58, 174
Republicans, 11, 27, 30–31, 49, 58, 181, 184, 235
Reverse racism, 160
Robotics, 233
Romney, Mitt, 58
Russell, Bertrand, 54
Russia, 28, 30–31, 154, 193, 214, 216, 246

S

Sagan, Carl, 1, 15, 249
Scientist's spirituality, 11
Scientology, 124
Self-interest, 29, 40–42, 46–48, 51, 59, 193, 198, 211–212, 215, 244
Semmelweis, Ignaz, 110
Shapiro, Ben, 186, 189
Shareholders, 199–200
Shia, 151, 207
Shia Muslims, 151, 207
Skepticism, 136
Sledgehammer, 64, 66–67
Smith, Adam, 190
Smith, Will, 218
Social programs, 46, 67, 78, 81, 108, 191
Social Security, 162, 179, 186–192
Socialism, 190–192
Societal Contexts, 88, 97, 99, 101–103, 105, 123, 125, 127, 129, 155
Soros, George, 26
Spiritual tribe, 47
Squatters, 179–181, 189–190, 202
Stark, Aaron, 22, 24, 32, 94, 96, 223, 231
Sunni Muslims, 207–208

T

Thank You for Arguing, 33
Toxic masculinity, 224
Tribal behavior, 7, 11
Tribalism, 1–7, 9–13, 15, 21, 25, 28, 30–31, 190, 192, 207, 233–236
Trolley problem, 152–154
Trump, Donald, 26, 53, 58, 60, 70, 162, 171–172, 174
Twain, Mark, 131
Type of government, 108
Tyson, Neil DeGrasse, 75, 233, 237

U

Ukraine, 28–29, 204–205, 214, 216, 241
Universal basic income (UBI), 67, 191
Universe, 14, 65–66, 123, 140, 142–143, 146–147, 160, 229, 233, 237–238
Unnecessary Enemies, 158, 162
Upper management, 43–45
US, 11, 16, 28, 41, 156, 190, 193, 200, 203, 209, 212–216, 235–236, 246, 249

V

Violence, 4, 7, 20, 32, 53, 79 98, 173, 207–208, 218, 224
violent conflict, 151–152
violent criminal behavior, 136
Voter fraud, 49

W

Wealth level, 71, 108
West, Cornel, 163
White people, 61, 78, 94, 100, 133–137, 151, 157–162
White tribe, 47
Work ethic, 108, 222
World War II, 205, 213

X

Xenophobia, 109
Xenophobic dimension, 163

Z

Zoroastrianism, 123

www.ingramcontent.com/pod-product-compliance
Lightning Source LLC
Chambersburg PA
CBHW060455030426
42337CB00015B/1593